How to Read the Church Fathers

*Every time a Christian renewal has blossomed in our West,
whether in thought or in life (and the two are always linked),
it has blossomed under the sign of the Fathers.*

Henri de Lubac

*Being faithful to the tradition
is not a matter of repeating theological theses and
transmitting them literally;
rather, it is a matter of imitating our fathers in the faith,
an attitude of intimate reflection and the effort of bold
creation,
necessary preludes to true spiritual fidelity.*

Hans Urs von Balthasar

Adalbert Hamman

How to Read the Church Fathers

SCM PRESS LTD

Translated by John Bowden and Margaret Lydamore from the French
Pour lire les Pères de l'Église,
published 1991 by Les Éditions du Cerf,
29 bd Latour-Maubourg, Paris

Maps by John Flower

334 02090 5

First published in English 1993
by SCM Press Ltd, 26–30 Tottenham Road, London N1 4BZ

Typeset at The Spartan Press Ltd, Lymington, Hants
and printed in Great Britain by
Butler & Tanner Ltd, Frome and London

Contents

A Church Father's Identity Card

- Converted in adulthood
- University education (usually)
- Experience of monastic life (often)
- Was made pastor of a church, or at least a priest
- Characteristics (according to Vincent of Lérins)
  Outstanding doctrine and orthodoxy, holiness, antiquity (i.e. the fathers
  date from the first five centuries)

A Brief Glossary

Father: among the Jews, the name given to someone who taught scripture;
among Christians, someone who nourished faith: first of all a bishop, then,
among the desert fathers, someone who trained disciples.

Church father: commonly used of ancient Christian writers, who are distinguished by the brilliance of their teaching. Ancient Christian writers up to
Isidore of Seville (who died in 636) are known as church fathers.

Patrology: another name for ancient Christian literature (or a book containing
information about the church fathers).

Patristics (short for 'patristic theology'): the study of theology and the history of
the doctrines of the fathers.

Definitions

Ascetic: someone who has renounced marriage.

Monk: someone who lives alone (without a wife). Hence,

Monastery: the place where monks live, and

Monasticism: the state of those who dedicate themselves completely to God.

Hermit: someone who lives in the desert. Synonymous with

Anchorite: someone who retires from the world in order to live alone.

Cenobite: someone who lives in a community.
There are therefore two forms of the religious life: the solitary life of the
anchorite, and the communal life of the cenobite.

Abba (apa): means father, superior, hence abbot.

Amma: mother superior, hence abbess.

Introduction

The basin which contains the Mediterranean Sea is an enormous highway of communication from East to West, from Great Britain to the Tigris and Euphrates, the rivers which irrigate present-day Iraq. A first line of communication, from Jerusalem to Rome, splits in two, and goes through Greece on one side and North Africa on the other. This was the route of evangelization in the first century.

A second line begins from Antioch, in Syria, and goes as far as Gaul, present-day France. This is the road which brought Irenaeus to Lyons, by way of Rome, in the second century. A third begins from Antioch and reaches Alexandria, then Carthage and Rome. The message of the gospel and Christian doctrine were established in these great cities during the third century.

A fourth line goes in opposite directions from Antioch: in one across Cappadocia (Turkey) to Nisibis and Edessa; in the other westwards, meeting the Danube, crossing northern Italy and extending to Bordeaux and Poitiers in France. This region was evangelized in the fourth and fifth centuries.

The Christian writers of antiquity lived within this network. The leading evangelists and Christian thinkers wrote using the languages of the day: Greek (in the East), Syriac (in Eastern Syria) and Latin (in Africa, Gaul and Italy).

How to read a text

It must be remembered that on first reading an ancient text we may find it very strange: there is a difference in vocabulary, in culture and in sensitivity. This book will help you to give a context to the author and his surroundings. Once you have done that, it is always useful to follow a simple pattern:

1. Read the text slowly and attentively
2. Look for the link between ideas
3. Pick out technical, difficult, essential words
4. Write a summary of the important ideas.

The Confession of Faith

From the beginning, the church has presented the faith by means of a summarized exposition called a confession, profession, rule of faith, symbol. All the terms are synonymous, but they have nuances which we must first of all analyse.

1. *Confession* is a bibilical term which means 'to proclaim one's faith in the God of Israel'.

2. The *rule of faith* or the rule of truth is a more developed formula which, according to Irenaeus and Tertullian, expresses 'the faith which the church universal has received from the apostles and their disciples' (Irenaeus, *Against All the Heresies* I.1). This is a criterion which allows a distinction between false interpretations of the scriptures and true ones.

3. The term *symbol*, which is used in the context of baptism or of belief, does not have the usual meaning of 'figure' or 'sign', but comes from a Greek word meaning 'put together'. In early times, amongst the Greeks and Latins, the Greek *symbolon* or Latin *tessera* was an object cut in two. The two parts, when put together, allowed the owners to recognize each other and to prove that a contract existed between them. The baptismal symbol is therefore the sign of recognition amongst those who confess the same faith.

The contents of the symbol express the essentials of the faith. Originally, it contained christological formulas to do with the resurrection, for instance 'Jesus is Lord' (Rom. 10.9; I Cor. 12.3; 15.3–5); sometimes these were filled out with a second term: faith 'in God and in Jesus Christ' (I Cor. 8.6; I Tim. 2.5; 5.13; II Tim. 4.1).

(a) Confession of Faith: The Apostolic Fathers

A christological formula: Ignatius of Antioch

Close your ears, then, to any talk that ignores Jesus Christ, of David's lineage, of Mary. He was really born, ate and drank; was really persecuted in the days of Pontius Pilate, was really crucified and died, in the sight of all heaven and earth and the under-world. He was really raised from the dead.

Letter to the Trallians, 9.1–2

A trinitarian formula: Ignatius of Antioch

Make a real effort to stand firmly by the orders of the Lord and the apostles, so that whatever you do, you may succeed in body and soul, in faith and love, with the Son, the Father, and the Spirit.

Letter to the Magnesians, 13.1

(b) The Rule of Faith: Irenaeus

We guard with care the faith which we have received from the church. Coming by the spirit of God, this is like some noble treasure in a precious vessel, continually reviving its youth and causing the vessel that holds it to revive in the same way.

For the church is entrusted with this gift of God, namely the Spirit, just as the breath of life was put in the work fashioned by his hands at the beginning of the world. So all the members could share in it and receive its life. In the church has been deposited communion with Christ, i.e. the Holy Spirit, the pledge of incorruption, the confirmation of our faith, and the ladder by which we ascend to God. For in the church, as Paul writes, God has set apostles, prophets, teachers and all the other work-ings of the Spirit. None of those who refuse to join the church partake of this Spirit, depriving them-selves of life by their evil views and intolerable actions. For where the church is, there also is the Spirit of God; and where the Spirit of God is, there is the church, and all grace. And the Spirit is truth.

Irenaeus, *Against All the Heresies*, III.24

Tertullian

The rule of faith is absolutely one, open to neither change nor reform:

> To believe in one Almighty God, creator of the world, and in one Son, Jesus Christ, born of the Virgin Mary, crucified under Pontius Pilate, who rose again on the third day, was received into heaven from the dead and now sits at the right hand of the Father, from whence he will come to judge the living and the dead, and also in the resurrection of the flesh.
> *On the Veiling of Virgins*, 1

The rule of faith is that by which we believe that there is but one God, who is none other than the Creator of the world, who produced everything from nothing by his Word; that this Word is called his Son who was brought down by the Spirit and Power of God into the Virgin Mary; was crucified, on the third day rose again, was caught up into heaven and sat down at the right hand of the Father; that he will come to judge the wicked to everlasting fire, with the restoration of their flesh.

Prescriptions against Heretics, 13

(c) The baptismal symbol

A legend

A legend which goes back to the fourth century tells how the Twelve, before scattering, each formulated one of the twelve articles which made up the symbol or creed, hence its name Apostles' Creed. Rufinus is the first to relate it (*Commentary on the Apostles' Creed*, 2). A sermon from Gaul, attributed to St Augustine, tells us precisely which article was contributed by each apostle.

This legend undoubtedly just seeks to illustrate the affirmation which we have already met in the 'rule of faith', that the truth confessed at baptism comes from all the apostles. *The Letter to the Apostles*, an apocryphal writing from the middle of the second century, provides us with the first text of a baptismal symbol (or creed) made up of five articles:

> I believe in the Father, Lord of all,
> and in Jesus Christ (our Saviour),
> and in the Holy Spirit (the Paraclete),
> and in the holy church,
> and in the forgiveness of sins.

An engraving from the Catacomb of Priscilla

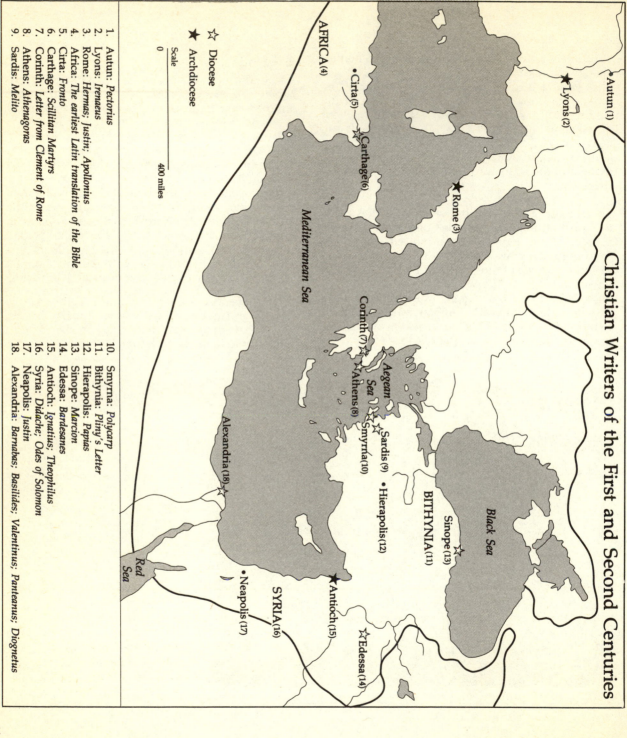

Christian Writers of the First and Second Centuries

☆ Diocese

★ Archdiocese

Scale

0 _____ 400 miles

AFRICA (4)

• Cirta (5)

☆ Carthage (6)

★ Rome (3)

Mediterranean Sea

Corinth (7) ☆

Aegean Sea

☆ Athens (8)

Sardis (9) ☆

☆ Smyrna (10)

• Hierapolis (12)

BITHYNIA (11)

Sinope (13) ☆

Black Sea

Alexandria (18) ☆

• Neapolis (17)

SYRIA (16)

★ Antioch (15)

☆ Edessa (14)

Red Sea

• Autun (1)

★ Lyons (2)

1. Autun: *Pectorius*
2. Lyons: *Irenaeus*
3. Rome: *Hermas; Justin; Apollonius*
4. Africa: *The earliest Latin translation of the Bible*
5. Cirta: *Fronto*
6. Carthage: *Scillitan Martyrs*
7. Corinth: *Letter from Clement of Rome*
8. Athens: *Athenagoras*
9. Sardis: *Melito*

10. Smyrna: *Polycarp*
11. Bithynia: *Pliny's Letter*
12. Hierapolis: *Papias*
13. Sinope: *Marcion*
14. Edessa: *Bardesanes*
15. Antioch: *Ignatius; Theophilus*
16. Syria: *Didache; Odes of Solomon*
17. Neapolis: *Justin*
18. Alexandria: *Barnabas; Basilides; Valentinus; Pantaenus; Diognetus*

1

From Jerusalem to Rome

The two routes taken by Peter and Paul ended up in Rome, where the apostles encountered a Christian community already sufficiently important to be noticed and to provoke their persecution. The leader of the apostles had above all been in contact with Jewish Christians. When he left Antioch, Paul had undertaken three journeys, which enabled him to carry the gospel to the main centres from Asia Minor as far as Greece.

I · The Birth of Christian Letters

The first writings, such as the Letter of Clement, are contemporary with and perhaps even earlier than the last works of the New Testament. From the outset, different cultures made themselves felt. At first they were dovetailed, but soon developed in parallel.

The southern route, from Jerusalem to Rome through Alexandria and Africa, went through towns where Judaism was firmly established. The Christian community took the organization of the synagogue as its model. The northern route left Antioch and went towards Greece, going through Asia Minor. Then the apostle to the nations followed the main thoroughfares and planted the cross in the most important centres: Ephesus, Corinth, Thessalonica. The converts came mostly from the pagan world, from Greek culture.

1. Judaeo–Christian writings

The Jews who joined the church kept their own traditions within it. Abraham remained their father and the Bible was their book, which had blazed the trail for the gospel. They also brought writings which were to be called apocryphal; these proliferated at this period, and people did not hesitate to cram them with Christian interpolations. We find such interpolations in, for instance, the Book of Enoch or the Sybilline Oracles.

The church kept the forms of Jewish prayer: confession of faith, doxology, psalms, messianic prophecies. The early liturgy took its inspiration from the synagogue. The baptismal rite borrowed from the baptism of proselytes; the eucharist, still associated with an actual meal, used Jewish prayers

1

I Peter written on a square papyrus, from the third century. This is the earliest manuscript of the text, which was preserved in the sands of Egypt. It was presented by Martin Bodmer to Pope Paul VI and is in the Vatican Library

at meals, which are to be found in the Didache. The same book mentions the ministries existing in the synagogues: prophets and teachers (13; 5). To them must be added presbyters (elders), who corporately supervised the Jewish–Christian communities.

The writings which came out of this background were composed within the biblical sphere of influence. The Odes of Solomon come close to the inspiration of the psalmists; the Shepherd of Hermas copies Jewish apocalyptic and preserves its images and symbols; the Didache, like the Letter of Barnabas, gives us a description of 'the two ways', known today through the texts of Qumran.

The Didache

The first guide for missionaries in the Jewish–Christian world, the Didache went through several revisions. It follows the stages of catechesis and has a doctrinal part and a liturgical part. The book is arranged into the following sections: the two ways, baptism, fasting, prayer, the eucharist. Instructions on the liturgy describe the organization of the church, house meetings, and preparation for the return of Christ with the prayer *maranatha* (Come, Lord), preserved in Aramaic.

The Letter of Barnabas, or the key to scripture

This is an anonymous text, fictitiously attributed to the apostle Barnabas, which recalls the communities at Damascus and Qumran. In it we find traces of baptismal initiation (6, 11), an allusion to the celebration of Sunday, and above all a christological interpretation of Old Testament values: circumcision, the temple, the sabbath. An allegorical reading of scripture, dear to the Alexandrians from Philo to Origen, was considered to be the only true one. Today the Christian community is the temple:

'God truly dwells in us in whom he has made his dwelling' (16.8).

The Shepherd of Hermas

The book which bears the title Shepherd purports to be the work of a certain Hermas, a brother of Pope Pius (140–155). The book enjoyed such a reputation in the East that it was sometimes numbered amongst the books of Holy Scripture.

Visions, precepts, parables follow one after the other, using apocalyptic imagery; the symbolism is sometimes disconcerting, but sublime. For instance, there is the old woman, or the tower, which stand for the church. The Shepherd gives a realistic picture of a community where good and evil live cheek by jowl. Material considerations, weakness, laziness and persecution have led to the falling away and even apostasy of some people.

The book is above all a call to penitence. Penitence even allows the sinner to find his place again, like a stone in the building of the church. The completion of the church will come at the end of time.

The Odes of Solomon, or the first Christian poetry

This collection of forty-two odes has been fictitiously attributed to king Solomon. The work is undoubtedly Christian, but would be found familiar by a Jewish Christian. So here is the first poetic work from the church, influenced by semitic thought and poetry (for example, it uses the technique of parallelism, which is so characteristic of the Psalms).

Here an archaic theology develops themes such as the epic of the victorious Christ, the descent into Hell, the virgin birth, the evocation of baptismal water, the return to paradise. And the Christian life is seen as a nuptial union.

Didache – Eucharistic Prayers

Now about the Eucharist: This is how to give thanks:
First in connection with the cup:

We thank you, our Father,
for the holy vine of David, your servant,
which you have revealed through Jesus, your child.
To you be glory for ever.

Then in connection with the piece broken off the loaf:

We thank you, our Father,
for the life and knowledge which you have revealed through Jesus, your child.
To you be glory for ever.

As this piece of bread was scattered over the hills
and then was brought together and made one,
so let your church be brought together from the ends of the earth into your kingdom.

For yours is the glory and the power through Jesus Christ for ever.

After you have finished your meal, say grace in this way:

We thank you, holy Father, for your sacred name
which you have lodged in our hearts, and for the knowledge and faith and immortality
which you have revealed through Jesus, your child.

To you be glory for ever.

Almighty Master, you have created everything for the sake of your name,
and have given men food and drink to enjoy that they may thank you.
But to us you have given spiritual food and drink and eternal life through Jesus, your child.
Above all we thank you that you are mighty. To you be glory for ever.

Remember, Lord, your Church, to save it from all evil and to make it perfect by your love.
Make it holy, and gather it together from the four winds into your kingdom which you have
made ready for it.
For yours is the power and the glory for ever.

Let Grace come and let this world pass away.
Hosanna to the God of David!
If anyone is holy, let him come. If not, let him repent.
Marana tha! Amen.

chs. 9; 10

Shepherd of Hermas: The building of the tower of penitence

When she had said this she wished to go away, but I fell at her feet and begged her by the Lord to show me the vision which she had promised. So she again took me by the hand and lifted me up, and made me sit on the couch on the left while she herself sat on the right. Then she lifted up a glittering rod and said to me, 'Do you see a great thing?' I said to her, 'Lady, I see nothing.' She said to me, 'Do you not see before you a great tower being built on the water with shining square stones?' Now the tower was being built four-square by the six young men who had come with her; but tens of thousands of other men were bringing stones, some from the deep sea, and some from the land, and were giving them to the six young men, and these kept taking them and building. The stones which had been dragged from the deep sea they placed without exception as they were into the building, for they had all been shaped and fitted into the joins with the other stones. And they so fastened one to the other that their joins could not be seen. But the building of the tower appeared as if it had been built of a single stone. Of the other stones, which were being brought from the dry ground, they cast some away, and some they put into the building and others they broke up and cast far from the tower. And many other stones were lying round the tower, and they did not use them for the building, for some of them were rotten, and others had cracks. And others were too short, and others were white and round and did not fit into the building.

When she had shown me these things, the old lady wanted to hasten away. I said to her: 'Lady, what does it benefit me to have seen these things, if I do not know what they mean?' – 'Hear then,' she said, 'the parables of the tower, for I will reveal everything to you. And do not trouble me about revelation any longer, for these revelations are finished, because they have been fulfilled. But you will not stop asking for revelations, since you are shameless.

The tower which you see being built is myself, the church, who have appeared to you both now and formerly. So ask what you will about the tower, and I will reveal it to you, so that you may rejoice with the saints.

Listen, then, concerning the stones which go into the building. The stones which are square and white and which fit into their joins are the apostles and bishops and teachers and deacons who walked according to the majesty of God, and served the elect of God in holiness and reverence as bishops and teachers and deacons; some of them have fallen asleep and some are still alive. And they always agreed among themselves, and had peace among themselves, and listened to one another; for which cause their joins fit in the building of the tower. But who are they who agree in their joins with the other stones which have already been built? These are the ones which have suffered for the name of the Lord. But who are those whom they were rejecting and throwing away? These are the ones who have sinned and wish to repent; for this reason they have not been thrown far from the tower, because they will be valuable for the building if they repent. Those, then, who are going to repent, if they do so, will be strong in the faith if they repent now, while the tower is being built; but once the building is finished, they will no longer have a place, but will be cast away. All that will be left to them is that they lie beside the tower.

Visions III, 3, 2–5

The Odes of Solomon

My heart was pruned and its flower appeared,
then grace sprang up in it and bore fruit for the Lord.
The Most High cut me with his Holy Spirit,
he uncovered my innermost being and filled me with his love,
and his wounding became my salvation.

I ran on the way in his peace,
on the way of truth, from beginning to end.
I received his knowledge,
and I was established upon the rock of truth where he had set me.

Speaking water touched my lips,
coming from the Lord's generous spring.
I drank and became intoxicated with the living water that does not die.
My intoxication was not a loss of reason, but I abandoned vanity.

I turned toward the Most High, my God, and was enriched by his generosity.
I abandoned the folly of the earth, stripped it off and cast it from me.
And the Lord renewed me with his garment, and possessed me by his light.

From on high he gave me immortal rest,
I became like the land which shoots, blossoms and bears fruits.
Like the sun upon the face of the land, the Lord lightened my eyes.
My countenance received the dew, and my breath tasted fragrance of the Lord.

He transported me to his Paradise, wherein is the wealth and pleasure of the Lord.
I lay prostrate before the Lord because of his glory, and said to him:
Blessed, Lord, are those who are planted in your land, and who find a place in your Paradise;
who grow in the plantation of your trees, and have passed from darkness to light.
Behold, all your labourers are excellent,
they work good works,
and turn from wickedness to your kindness.
They have rejected the bitterness of the trees, when they were planted in your land.

All your land is like a remnant of you
and an eternal remembrance of your faithful works.
There is much room in your Paradise;
nothing in it is barren, and all is filled with fruits.

Glory be to you, O God,
the delight of Paradise for ever.
Hallelujah!

Ode 11

2. The first pastoral letters: the missionary church

Thanks to the efforts of the apostle Paul, there were now many Christian communities made up of former pagans. They understood the gospel message in Hellenistic terms. Their language was Greek, the international language of the whole of the Mediterranean basin.

The first writings to come from these new communities had more in common with life than literature. They were the letters of pastors: Clement, Bishop of Rome; Ignatius, Bishop of Antioch; Polycarp, Bishop of Smyrna; and Papias of Hierapolis (said to have made a collection of sayings of the Lord).

Letters were links between the communities, between countries, and between the pastor and the faithful. The churches wrote to one another as a mark of their unity, and the pastors kept up a correspondence among themselves and with the communities which ranged from information to exhortation. The first letters came from bishops who at this period were the leaders above all of communities which Paul had founded, working with deacons as assistants. Between the period when churches were organized like synagogues and the time when they came under bishops, there was a period of flux, which was resolved through association and integration.

Clement of Rome writes to Corinth

This is the first Christian writing, composed around the year 96, at the time when the apostle John was still living at Ephesus. The Roman church sent three delegates who brought the letter to Corinth, to assert their community's authority. Although he is never named, Clement was its author. He intervened in a turbulent community in which the young people had dismissed the experienced members of the college of presbyters. He wrote as someone who expected to be obeyed.

Ignatius of Antioch

The difference between Paul and Ignatius, as the great patristic scholar Jean Daniélou points out, 'is like that between a missionary who adapts himself to the natives and a native who rethinks Christianity'. Coming from humble origins, Ignatius succeeded Evodius as Bishop of Antioch, the largest city in Syria, at the beginning of the second century, when the church was fifty years old. Originally a pagan and influenced by philosophy, he knew the procedure of Stoic diatribe as well as the sophistications of Asian rhetoric.

He was arrested around 110 and taken under a military escort to Rome. There he was not beheaded, but thrown to the wild beasts for food. On his travels he showed a concern for all the churches through which he passed. He wrote seven letters to them which have survived (to the Ephesians, the Magnesians, the Trallians, the Philadelphians, the Smyrnaeans and Polycarp). The most important, the one sent to the Romans before

---

Clement of Rome to the Corinthians

The resurrection to come

Let us consider, dear friends, how the Master continually points out to us that there will be a future resurrection. Of this he made the Lord Jesus Christ the first fruits by raising him from the dead.

Let us take note, dear friends, of the resurrection at the natural seasons. Day and night demonstrate resurrection. Night passes and day comes. Day departs and night returns. Take the crops as examples. How and in what way is the seeding done? The sower goes out and casts each of his seeds in the ground. When they fall on the ground they are dry and bare, and they decay. But then the marvellous providence of the Master resurrects them from their decay, and from a single seed many grow and bear fruit.

I Clement, 24

The Main Ancient Religions

Cybele

Goddess of ancient Phrygia, 'mother of the gods' and goddess of fertility. Celebrated at Ephesus. The cult was brought to Rome before 204 BC and was often linked with that of Attis.

Manichaeanism

This was the religion preached by Mani (216–277). It arose in Mesopotamia and spread into the Far East and the West. It is based on two main antagonists, light and darkness (cf. Aphraat, Ephraem, Cyril of Jerusalem, Serapion and Augustine).

Mithras

An Iranian god, of Indo-Persian origin (1300 BC). His cult spread through Asia Minor and in the Roman Empire (first century AD). This was an astral religion with a festival of the *deus invinctus* (invincible God), celebrated in the winter solstice. When Christianized, the festival became Christmas (25 December: cf. Justin, Tertullian, Origen).

Mystery religions

These were organized and practised by men and women initiated into associations. There they practised secret rites which allowed them to enter into communion with their god. The main Greek mysteries were those of Eleusis and the Orphic Mysteries (but also Attis, Isis, Cybele and Mithras, cf. Justin).

Greek and Roman religion

This was an anthopomorphic polytheism which cultivated the pantheon of gods: twelve Olympian deities and then a host of gods and goddesses, and lastly inferior deities who served the others (like Iris, the messenger of Zeus). The Romans identified the Greek deities with their own, so that Zeus became Jupiter (cf. Justin and Augustine). The philosophers rejected this mythology.

he came to know them, expresses in enigmatic language the mystic passion which burned in him: 'There is no fire left in me for the matter; only a living water murmurs inside me and says to me: Come to the Father!'

The Letters of Ignatius are one of the jewels of Christian literature, among the most important pieces of ancient history, rich in information on the life of the churches.

The bishop confesses the faith as he received it from the apostles. And his teaching is extremely clear on the humanity and divinity of Christ, which he defends against those who play down their reality. He warned against those who 'Judaize' and revert to observances which he considers obsolete.

The most important concept in his doctrine is unity: the unity of God, one and three; the unity of Christ in the duality of his two natures; the unity of the Christian with Christ, foundation of the spiritual life; and the unity of Christians with one another in the church, of which the visible sign is the bishop, surrounded by priests who form a senate and by deacons who through social service express 'the *diaconia* (service) of Jesus Christ'.

The Heddernheim Table
(illustration from F. Cumont,
Textes et monuments relatifs aux
mystères de Mithra, 1896)

Ignatius to the Smyrnaeans

Follow the bishop

You should all follow the bishop as Jesus Christ followed the Father. Follow, too, the presbytery as you would the apostles; respect your deacons as you would God's law. Nobody must take any step that has to do with the church without the bishop's approval. The only eucharist to be regarded as valid is one that is celebrated by the bishop himself, or by someone authorized by him. Where the bishop is present, there let the congregation gather, just as wherever Jesus Christ is present, there is the Catholic Church.

Ignatius, *To the Smyrnaeans*, 8

The Martyrdom of Polycarp

They set about him the material prepared for the pyre. And when they were about to nail him also, he said: 'Leave me as I am. For he who grants me to endure the fire will enable me also to remain on the pyre unmoved, without the security you desire from the nails.'

So they did not nail him, but tied him. And with his hands put behind him and tied, like a noble ram out of a great flock ready for sacrifice, a burnt offering ready and acceptable to God, he looked up to heaven and said:

Lord God Almighty, Father of your beloved and blessed servant Jesus Christ, through whom we have received full knowledge of you, the God of angels and powers and all creation and of the whole race of the righteous who live in your presence,

I bless you because you have thought me worthy of this day and hour, to take my part in the number of the martyrs, in the cup of your Christ, for resurrection to eternal life of soul and body in the immortality of the Holy Spirit.

May I be received among them in your presence this day as a rich and acceptable sacrifice, just as you have prepared and revealed beforehand and fulfilled, you who are the true God without any falsehood. For this and for everything I praise you, I bless you, I glorify you, through the eternal and heavenly High Priest, Jesus Christ, your beloved servant.

Through him be glory to you with him and the Holy Spirit both now and to the ages to come. Amen.

When he had said the Amen and finished his prayer, the men attending to the fire lighted it. And when the flame flashed forth, we saw a miracle, we to whom it was given to see. And we are preserved in order to relate to the rest what happened. For the fire made the shape of a vaulted chamber, like a ship's sail filled by the wind, and made a wall around the body of the martyr. And he was in the midst, not as burning flesh, but as bread baking or as gold and silver refined in a furnace. And we perceived such a sweet aroma as the breath of incense or some other precious spice.

The Martyrdom of Polycarp, 13, 14, 15

Ignatius of Antioch to the Romans

I am writing to all the churches and bidding them all realize that I am voluntarily dying for God – if, that is, you do not interfere. I plead with you, do not do me an untimely kindness. Let me be fodder for wild beasts – that is how I can get to God. I am God's wheat and I am being ground by the teeth of wild beasts to make a pure loaf for Christ. I would rather that you fawn on the beasts so that they may be my tomb and no scrap of my body be left. Thus, when I have fallen asleep, I shall be a burden to no one. Then I shall be a real disciple of Jesus Christ when the world sees my body no more. Pray Christ for me that by these means I may become God's sacrifice. I do not give you orders like Peter and Paul. They were apostles: I am a convict. They were at liberty: I am still a slave. But if I suffer, I shall be emancipated by Jesus Christ; and united to him, I shall rise to freedom.

Even now as a prisoner, I am learning to forgo my own wishes. All the way from Syria to Rome I am fighting with wild beasts, by land and sea, night and day, chained as I am to ten leopards (I mean to a detachment of soldiers), who only get worse the better you treat them. But by their injustices I am becoming a better disciple, though not for that reason am I acquitted. What a thrill I shall have from the wild beasts that are ready for me! I hope they will make short work of me. I shall coax them on to eat me up at once and not to hold off, as sometimes happens, through fear. And if they are reluctant, I shall force them to it. Forgive me – I know what is good for me. Now is the moment I am beginning to be a disciple. May nothing seen or unseen begrudge me making my way to Jesus Christ. Come fire, cross, battling with wild beasts, wrenching of bones, mangling of limbs, crushing of my whole body, cruel tortures of the devil – only let me get to Jesus Christ!

Not the wide bounds of earth nor the kingdoms of this world will avail me anything. I would rather die and get to Jesus Christ than reign over the ends of the earth. That is whom I am looking for – the one who died for us. That is whom I want – the one who rose for us. I am going through the pangs of being born. Sympathize with me, my brothers. Do not stand in the way of my coming to life – do not wish death on me. Do not give back to the world one who wants to be God's: do not trick him with material things. Let me get into the clear light and manhood will be mine. Let me imitate the passion of my God. If anyone has Him in him, let him appreciate what I am longing for, and sympathize with me, realizing what I am going through.

The prince of this world wants to kidnap me and pervert my godly purpose. None of you, then, who will be there, must abet him. Rather be on my side – that is, on God's. Do not talk Jesus Christ and set your heart on the world. Harbour no envy. If, when I arrive, I make a different plea, pay no attention to me. Rather heed what I am now writing to you. For though alive, it is with a passion for death that I am writing to you. My desire has been crucified and there burns in me no passion for material things. There is living water in me, which speaks and says inside me, 'Come to the Father.' I take no delight in corruptible food or in the dainties of this life. What I want is God's bread, which is the flesh of Christ, who came from David's line; and for drink I want his blood: an immortal love feast indeed.

I do not want to live any more on a human plane. And so it shall be, if you want it to. Want it to, so that you will be wanted. Despite the brevity of my letter, trust my request. Yes, Jesus Christ will clarify it for you and make you see I am really in earnest. He is the guileless mouth by which the Father has spoken truthfully. Pray for me that I reach my goal.

Ignatius, *To the Romans*, 4, 5, 6, 7, 8

CHRONOLOGICAL TABLE

	Popes	Emperors	
Peter (30?–64)	Lucius (253–254)	Tiberius (14–37)	Valerian (253–260)
Linus (64?–76?)	Stephen (254–257)	Caligula (37–41)	Gallian (260–268)
Anacletus (76?–88?)	Sixtus II (257–258)	Claudius (41–54)	Aurelian (270–275)
Clement (88?–c.100)	Dionysius (259–268)	Nero (54–68)	Diocletian (284–305)
Evaristus (?–?)	Felix (270–275)	Vespasian (69–79)	Maximian
Alexander (?–?)	Eutychian (275–283)	Titus (79–81)	Tetrachy
Sixtus (?–?)	Gaius (283–296)	Domitian (81–96)	Constantine-Licinius
Telesphorus (?–c.136)	Marcellinus (296–204)	Trajan (98–117)	Constantine (306–337)
Hyginus (c.136–c.140)	Eusebius (309–310)	Hadrian (117–138)	Constans (337–350)
Pius (c.140–before 154)	Sylvester (314–335)	Antoninus (138–162)	Constantius (361)
Anicetus (from 154–?)	Julius (337–352)	Marcus Aurelius (162–180)	Julian (361–363)
Soter (before 175–175)	Liberius (352–366)	Commodus (180–192)	Valentinian I (364–375)
Eleutherus (175–189)	Damasus (366–384)	Septimus Severus (193–211)	Gratian (375–383)
Victor (189–199)	Siricius (384–399)	Caracalla (211–217)	Valentinian II (383–392)
Zephyrinus (199–217)	Innocent (401–417)	Severus Alexander (222–235)	Theodosius (395)
Callistus (217–222)	Celestine (422–432)	Maximin (235–238)	Valentinian III (395–423)
Urban (221–230)	Leo (440–461)	Decius (249–251)	Honorius (425–455)
Pontian (230–235)	Symmachus (498–514)		
Anterus (235–236)	Vigilius (537–555)		
Fabian (236–250)	Gregory (590–604)		
Cornelius (251–253)			

II · The Encounter between Faith and Culture: The Apologists

The second century was a period of great missionary expansion. From the Mediterranean and other coastal regions the church spread into the interior, in Asia Minor, in Egypt and in Africa. Pliny the Younger found numerous Christians as far away as the shores of the Black Sea. In 177 the Bishop of Lyons, Pothinus, was a nonagenarian, his episcopate having begun thirty years earlier. From the capital of the Gauls, the gospel spread through Germania, to Trier and Cologne.

From then on, in the great cities of Antioch and Alexandria the religion of Christ embraced all levels of society, workers and people of low birth as well as educated people, rhetoricians and philosophers. At first the church was somewhat taken by surprise and found itself ill-prepared to enter into dialogue with Greek thought, and to express its faith in Hellenistic concepts and language.

Three tasks awaited those whom we call the apologists, who from this time on are skilled writers: to defend Christianity against the common misrepresentations and the accusations of the philosophers; to refute the charges of idolatry and polytheism while affirming belief in the one God revealed in Jesus Christ; and finally to present the Christian faith in a language and in concepts accessible to educated people.

We know little about some of these apologists. Only their names or brief fragments have come down to us: for instance, Athenagoras' treatise *On the Resurrection of the Dead*. The author of the Epistle to Diognetus is unknown to us. Along with the philosopher Athenagoras, the most famous and the most characteristic of them is certainly Justin, whose principal works have been preserved.

1. To Diognetus

We know neither the author, nor the date, nor the place of composition of this famous text. It is an apology for Christianity addressed to a pagan, and answers three questions which have been asked: What is the religion of Christians and why do they reject that of Jews and pagans? What does this brotherly love consist of, that they commend above all things? Why did Christ come so late?

The author replies to all these questions and expounds the place of Christians in the world: they are its soul, sharing fully in every condition of life while being at the same time citizens promised to another city: 'Every foreign land is their fatherland, and yet for them every fatherland is a foreign land.'

2. Justin, lay theologian

Born at Nablus in Palestine, near ancient Shechem, into a family of Greek-speaking settlers, he set about looking for a true philosophy. About 130, he was converted to Christianity: 'I recognized (in Christianity) that here was the only certain and beneficial philosophy.' After a stay at Ephesus he came to Rome and spent a long time there, always wearing the mantle of a philosopher; he founded a Christian school. He died a martyr's death in 165 with several of his disciples.

Works

Of Justin's works we still have the two Apologies and the Dialogue with Trypho the Jew.

The First Apology, addressed to the Emperor Antoninus (around 150) consists first of all of a defence of Christianity: Christians are neither atheists nor enemies of the state nor criminals. A second part justifies Christian truth, showing that Christ is the Son of God because he fulfils the prophecies. Finally, Justin describes Christian life and worship: baptism, the eucharist, the celebration of Sunday. His is the oldest description of the liturgy that we have.

A Phoenician ship portrayed on a
Roman sarcophagus

14

The Second Apology, addressed to the Roman Senate, seems to be mainly a rebuttal of attacks by the rhetorician Fronto, whom we know through the work Octavius by Minucius Felix (about 225).

The Dialogue with Trypho the Jew is the most important document on the controversy and dialogue between Christians and Jews, and on the efforts made to lead the latter to the faith of Christ. It is a long work. The structure is loose, and there are many digressions.

The work opens with an account of Justin's philosophical training and conversion (1–8). It goes on to demonstrate that the ancient law is abrogated; its role was to prepare for the new law. Justin shows his method of exegesis: for him the Old Testament is a sketch for and prophecy of the New, in its instructions and in the events which it records. Only Christianity provides the whole of humankind with the definitive and universal law.

Then, in a second part, he shows how, according to a miraculous preparatory law, all the prophecies find fulfilment in Christ, the Son of God, in whom the Father had already made himself known in the Old Testament (in theophanies). He suffered under Pontius Pilate, then he entered into the glory of his Father. And worship of Christ does not contradict the faith of Abraham, Isaac and Jacob in one God.

Doctrine

These controversies led to reflection on the Christian faith, a first theology of the Trinity and of Christ, God and humankind. However, this was not organized systematically. Justin highlighted the role of the Word (Logos) as distinct from the Father and yet coming from his substance without division, 'distinct by number, not by thought'.

This Word is the mediator between God and the world. Through him, God created and rules over the universe. He is at work in all that is true and good in the world. Everything that poets and philosophers know of truth is like a fragment of the Word sown in the world like a seed. 'Seeds of truth are to be found in everything.'

This Word which is already revealed in the theophanies of the Old Testament is fully revealed in Christ. The coming of the Messiah is at the heart of God's plan, and illuminates the whole of history. Justin outlines a first theology of history; and we know the importance it was to assume with Irenaeus of Lyons. This layman is the first theologian of the church: he demonstrates that only in Christianity are all the partial truths fulfilled. The Word invisibly guides the quest of all people for truth.

To Diognetus: The Soul of the World

To put it simply: What the soul is in the body, that Christians are in the world. The soul is dispersed through all the members of the body, and Christians are scattered through all the cities of the world. The soul dwells in the body, but does not belong to the body, and Christians dwell in the world, but do not belong to the world. The soul, which is invisible, is kept under guard in the visible body; in the same way, Christians are recognized when they are in the world, but their religion remains unseen. The flesh hates the soul and treats it as an enemy, even though it has suffered no wrong, because it is prevented from enjoying its pleasures; so too the world hates Christians, even though it suffers no wrong at their hands, because they range themselves against its pleasures. The soul loves the flesh that hates it, and its members; in the same way, Christians love those who hate them. The soul is shut up in the body, and yet itself holds the body together; while Christians are restrained in the world as in a prison, and yet themselves hold the world together. The soul, which is immortal, is housed in a mortal dwelling; while Christians are settled among corruptible things, to wait for the incorruptibility that will be theirs in heaven. The soul, when faring badly as to food and drink, grows better; so too Christians, when punished, day by day increase more and more. It is to no less a post than this that God has ordered them, and they must not try to evade it.

Epistle to Diognetus, 6

The Celebration of Sunday

After these services, we constantly remind each other of these things. Those who have more come to the aid of those who lack, and we are constantly together.[1] Over all that we receive we bless the Maker of all things through his Son Jesus Christ and through the Holy Spirit. And on the day called Sunday there is a meeting in one place of those who live in the cities or the country, and the memoirs of the apostles or the writings of the prophets are read as long as time permits. When the reader has finished, the president in a discourse urges and invites us to the imitation of these noble things. Then we all stand up together and offer prayers. And, as said before, when we have finished the prayer, bread is brought, and wine and water, and the president similarly sends up prayers and thanksgivings to the best of his ability, and the congregation assents, saying the Amen.

The distribution and reception of the consecrated elements by each one takes place, and they are sent to those absent by the deacons. Those who prosper, and who so wish, contribute, each one as much as he chooses to. What is collected is deposited with the president, and he takes care of orphans and widows, and those who are in want on account of sickness or any other cause, and those who are in bonds, and the strangers who are sojourners among us, and, briefly, he is the protector of all those in need.[2]

We all hold this common gathering on Sunday, since it is the first day, on which God, transforming darkness and matter, made the universe, and Jesus Christ our Saviour rose from the dead on the same day. For they crucified him on the day before Saturday, and on the day after Saturday he appeared to his apostles and disciples and taught them these things which I have passed on to you also for your serious consideration.

Justin, *First Apology*, 67

---

1. Mutual aid played an important role in the earliest community.
2. A preoccupation with the poor persists right through the first Christian literature.

Athenagoras: The Resurrection of the Dead

God did not make man in vain; for he is wise, and no work of wisdom is vain. But he did not make man for his own use; for he does not need anything, and in the case of one who has no needs at all, nothing which he has created can contribute anything to him for his own use. But neither did he make man for the sake of any other of his created works. For none of the beings, whether superior or inferior, who are gifted with reason and discernment, has been created or is created for the use of another but only for the continued survival of such creatures themselves. If man, then, was not created purposelessly or in vain (for nothing created by God is vain at least as far as the original intention of the creator is concerned), and was not created for the use of the Maker himself or any other of God's creations, it is clear that in terms of the primary and more general reason God made man for his own sake and out of the goodness and wisdom which is reflected throughout creation; but in terms of the reason which has a more immediate bearing on those created, God made man simply for the survival of such creatures themselves that they should not be kindled for a short time, then entirely extinguished. For God has assigned this fleeting form of life, I think, to snakes, birds, and fish, or, to speak more generally, to all irrational creatures; but the Maker has decreed an unending existence to those who bear his image in themselves, are gifted with intelligence, and share the faculty for rational discernment, so that they, knowing their Maker and his power and wisdom, and complying with law and justice, might live without distress eternally with the powers by which they governed their former life, even though they were in corruptible and earthly bodies.

Athenagoras, *On the Resurrection of the Dead*, 12

Philosophies

Aristotelianism

Also known as 'peripatetic' philosophy. It is named after Aristotle (384–322), who among other things was tutor to Alexander the Great, and based on observation and reason. God is the soul of the world, which is co-eternal with him. It exerted a limited influence over the ancient church.

Platonism

Plato was a disciple of Socrates (427–348), born in Athens. His idealist philosophy distinguishes between the world of the senses, which has no real value or permanence, and the world of Ideas, which alone has consistency. Only the soul is an emanation of the divinity, which it seeks to rediscover.

Philo was a Jewish philosopher (he died about AD 50), who made use of Platonism to interpret the Bible.

Plotinus (204–270) revised the system in Alexandria. For him man belongs to the tangible world through his body and to the divine world through his soul. He can rediscover this divine world by purification, meditation and ecstasy, thereby uniting himself with the one true being.

Stoicism

A Greek philosophy which goes back to Zeno (342–270), named after the portico (Stoa) in Athens, where it was taught. God is the active principle, the fiery spirit of the world. All human beings make up fragments of a homogenous Whole, ordered by a cosmic soul and ruled by immutable laws. Made up of four elements (fire, air, water, earth), the universe will come to an end in a cosmic conflagration. This was a philosophy whose moral severity influenced the first Christian generation, particularly Tertullian.

Judaism

Is divided into

– Jews:

- Palestinians: who live in the Holy Land (circumcised)
- Diaspora Jews, or Hellenists: Jews who are dispersed amongst the pagans

– Non-Jews:

- Proselytes: non-Jews integrated by circumcision and baptism
- God-fearers: non-Jews who accept monotheistic faith
- the uncircumcised, nations, Gentiles, pagans (a later, third-century term)

Jesus as seen by the Jewish historian Flavius Josephus, about AD 90

About this time arose Jesus, a wise man, if indeed it be lawful to call him a man. For he was a doer of wonderful deeds, and a teacher of men who gladly receive the truth. He drew to himself many of both the Jews and of the Gentiles. He was the Christ; and when Pilate, on the indictment of the principal men among us, had condemned him to the cross, those who had loved him at the first did not cease to do so; for he appeared to them alive on the third day, the prophets having foretold these and ten thousand other wonderful things about him.

Jewish Antiquities, 18.3.3

Heresies

Apollinarianism: the error of Apollinarius of Laodicea (fourth century), in which the Word of God takes the place of the human soul of Christ.

Arianism: the heresy of Arius, who denied the full divinity of Christ.

Gnosticism: heterodox systems which professed a deep-seated dualism between the world of spirits and the corporeal world, and affirmed the alleged revelation of emanations coming from a good God and an evil principle (the latter more or less identified with the material world) and manifesting themselves in the real world.

Manichaeism: the error of Manes (third century), which combines elements of Jewish and Christian heterodoxy to affirm a deep-seated dualism between a good principle and an evil one which are in conflict.

Marcionism: the error of Marcion (second century), who rejected the vengeful God of the Old Testament in favour of the good God revealed in Jesus Christ.

Montanism: the error of Montanus of Phrygia (second century), who taught an incarnation of the Holy Spirit in himself and an imminent return of Christ.

Monothelitism: a heresy which asserted that there was only one will (the divine one) in Christ.

Nestorianism: an error imputed to Nestorius which distinguished two natures in Christ to the point of seeing two persons in him.

Monophysitism: an error professed by Eutyches, a monk from Constantinople (fifth century), which allowed only one nature (the divine) in Christ, the divine nature absorbing the human nature.

Dictionary

Allegory: a text or image which conceals a hidden and deeper meaning. The image of the tower, in the *Shepherd*, symbolizes the church. According to Paul, Abraham's two wives stand for the synagogue and the church.

Apocalyptic: a literary genre which has as its object revelations or visions concerning the future (eschatology). It is expressed through a symbolic system in which colours and numbers mingle.

Apology: a written discourse seeking to defend or justify a person or a doctrine in the face of ill-informed interlocutors or detractors.

Codex: a document written in book format (as opposed to a scroll). The Latin word codex (translated code in English) denotes a summary of law, named after the person who inspired it: e.g. the Theodosian Code, the Justinian Code.

Diatribe: a procedure which presupposes a fictitious adversary, or a response to questions with fresh questions. A diatribe often resorts to personifications such as Sin, Death.

Economy: among Greek theologians, from the time of Irenaeus, denotes the plan of salvation among human beings unveiled by the coming and work of Christ.

Epectasis: according to Gregory of Nyssa, the tension between all that is finite and the infinite, between human beings and the fullness that God alone can satisfy, in a limitless growth.

Theology of history: a global interpretation of events and periods, in the light of Christ and his revelation.

Theophany: divine apparitions or visible manifestations of God, in human or angelic form. God appeared to Abraham as a visitor.

III · Irenaeus of Lyons (died about 200)

The Bishop of Lyons, who succeeded Pothinus in 177, and is known above all for his refutation of Gnosticism, is a guardian of the faith, a missionary for the gospel, a forerunner and a theologian who blazed a well-lit trail.

1. The crisis over Gnosticism

The name of the Bishop of Lyons is first and foremost associated with the Gnostic crisis. His major work is *Against All the Heresies*.

It is important to start by making a clear distinction between gnosis and Gnosticism. Gnosis, a Greek word meaning knowledge, is in no way suspect or heterodox. Judaism uses the term in the sense of experience rather than intellectual learning. That is the meaning it has in the prayer of the Didache.

For Clement of Alexandria, 'gnosis is the understanding of the gospel'. Irenaeus would have agreed with this definition, while at the same time reserving true gnosis for the church. But the true gnosis is forced to define itself over against false gnosis or the structures of Gnosticism.

Gnosticism comprises the doctrines of half-converted intellectuals, which swelled in number around 120–30. Far from accepting the faith, as Justin did, in accordance with the tradition of the apostles and of the church, they utilized and exploited it in terms of their philosophies and their doctrinal systems. Their legitimate thirst for knowledge became a rape of the divine mystery, and not a welcoming of it.

By the middle of the second century there was more Gnostic than orthodox literature, and it was increasing. It went into everything: the Bible, the apocryphal writings, theology and even poetry and prayer. The various types of Gnosticism spread around the area of the Black Sea and especially Alexandria – their hub – and extended as far as Rome, Carthage and eventually Lyons, the farthest point of Christendom.

2. The teaching of Irenaeus

Irenaeus' principal work is called *Against All the Heresies* or *The Refutation and Overthrow of the Knowledge Falsely So Called*, in five volumes. Later on he also wrote *The Demonstration of the Apostolic Preaching*, a kind of catechism of the Catholic faith.

Faced with the allegations from the various forms of Gnosticism, Irenaeus confined himself to what had been given through the Bible and the gospel teaching, received from the apostles and handed on by the rule of faith, a kind of résumé of essential truths. In opposition to the fundamental dualism of the Gnostics, he affirmed unity: one God, one Christ, one humankind, one church, one faith.

True gnosis

True gnosis teaches us not about the very mystery of God but about the creation, the work of his love for humankind, what Irenaeus, following St Paul, calls the economy (the organization), i.e. the divine plan which works through the history of salvation. The plan has its origin in the Trinity and leads humankind from its creation to its glorification in the vision of God.

Irenaeus' first certainty concerns God: there is no other God than the one who has created and moulded us. There is therefore no salvation outside him and his 'two hands', which are the Son and the Holy Spirit. The whole creation is the work of God; therefore it is good, including the material world, and ripe for salvation.

The economy and humankind

The creation of humankind takes place at the heart of the material world. A human being is not a spirit (Greek *pneuma*) fallen into a body, but a 'pneumatized' body, inhabited by the Holy Spirit, who is the guarantor of its unity and its incorruptibility. Human beings are made in the image of God, because in their very body they are made in the image of the Son, 'who was to be born as a human

The Roman theatre in Lyons

being'. The economy is humankind's slow and gradual climb, and the human responsibility in this climb towards perfect resemblance to God. Divine teaching consists in preparing human beings for God's visit, without scaring them off, getting them ready to welcome him and enter into communion with him.

The coming of Christ

So in early theology, the coming of Christ was in no way linked to sin but was 'foreseen from the beginning of the world'. The history of humankind has known failures – sin – resulting not from our corporeal nature (as the Gnostics would have it), but from our freedom and frailty, our lack of inclination to obedience. Like children, humankind grows up gradually and serves an apprenticeship in its responsibilities. Sin can thwart but not stand in the way of God's plan.

History appears as a gradual preparation for the coming of the Son, 'disseminated throughout the scriptures, speaking to Abraham, to Moses, to David'. God prepared the prophets to incline humankind to 'bear his Spirit and enter into communion with him'. For Irenaeus, Jesus is the luminous centre which illuminates the whole path of history. He acts as a model for the creation of humankind. 'Through the Incarnation, Christ brought God down in man through the Spirit; and Christ causes man to reach up to God, bringing to perfection in himself the work for which he is a model.'

In this way, Christ recapitulates in himself the long history of humankind from the first man, Adam. The cross of Christ, a replica of the tree of life, at the same time expresses the drama of his obedience, even unto death, nailed to the wood, 'to expiate the old disobedience but also to indicate by its fourfold shape that the cross embraces the universe' (*Apostolic Preaching*, 34).

The Spirit and the church

The economy of Christ is accomplished by the economy of the Spirit. The unction of the Spirit flows down from the Messiah over the whole body of the church and over each of its members. The Spirit dwells there and enfolds the church in its perfume: 'Where the church is, there the Spirit is; where the Spirit is, there is the church.'

The faith, sown in us, raises us in love and leads humankind to the vision of God. The eucharist is the last stage in the history of salvation. When consecrated, the bread and the wine, fruits of the earth, are the surge of the whole creation as it flows back to the Father from whom all gifts come. They celebrate thanksgiving and expectation, what is already present and the ripening of promises.

This is a splendid overall picture, which allowed Irenaeus to demonstrate the unity and progression of God's plan, the correspondence between the two Testaments, the two Adams, the two Eves (the original one and Mary), and the recapitulation of the whole of creation.

Irenaeus' Childhood Memories

His education from Bishop Polycarp in Smyrna

I remember events in those days better than recent happenings, since what we learn in childhood develops along with the mind and becomes a part of it. So I can describe the place where blessed Polycarp sat and talked, his comings in and goings out, his manner of life, his personal appearance, and the way in which he spoke to congregations. I remember how he spoke of his relations with John and the others who had seen the Lord; how he recalled their words and what he had heard them say about the Lord, his miracles and his teaching, things that he had heard directly from eyewitnesses to the Word of life. These he reported in complete accord with scripture. So by the mercy of God shown to me, I listened to these things eagerly at that time, not committing them to paper but learning them by heart. And again through the love of God I have truly ruminated on them, and I can bear witness before God that if this blessed and apostolic presbyter had heard any such suggestion (i.e. Gnostic doctrines), he would have cried out and stopped his ears, and would have remarked, as was his fashion, 'Dear God, for what times you have preserved me, that I should suffer this!' And he would have left the very place where he had been sitting or standing when he heard such words. One can also show this by the letters which he sent either to neighbouring churches to strengthen them, or to individual Christians to warn them and exhort them.

Letter from Irenaeus to Florinus, in Eusebius, *Church History*, v.20

Irenaeus in the year 160
(Hulton Deutsch)

Against Heresies

How then shall you be God when you are not yet made man? How shall you be made perfect when you are barely made at all? How shall you be immortal when you have not obeyed your Maker in your mortal nature? You must first guard carefully your position as man; only then will you partake in the glory of God. For it is not you who have made God, but God has made you. So if you are the work of God, wait patiently for the hand of your artist, who does all things in due season – and when I say 'in season' I mean in relation to you who are in the making. Offer him a supple and docile heart and keep the form which this artist has given you, having in yourself the Water that comes from him and without which, becoming hardened, you would lose the print of his fingers. By keeping this form, you will mount up to perfection, for by the art of God the clay which is in you will be concealed. His hand has created your substance; he will reclothe you with pure gold inside and out, and will so greatly adorn you that the king himself will desire your beauty. But if by becoming hard you reject his skill and show yourself discontent with the one who has made you man, by thus becoming unthankful to God, you have lost both his skill and your own life. For to make is proper to God's goodness and to be made is proper to man's nature. So if you present to him what is yours, i.e. faith in him and submission, you will receive the benefit of his art and you will be the perfect will of God.

If, on the contrary, you do not believe him, and flee from his hands, the cause of imperfection will be in yourselves, who did not obey, not in the one who called you. For he sent some to call men to the marriage, but those who did not obey him deprived themselves of the King's banquet.

So it is not God's skill which is at fault, since he can raise up sons to Abraham from stones; but those who do not bend to this art are the cause of their own imperfection. The light does not fail because of those who are themselves blind, but while it remains what it is, those who are blind are in darkness through their own fault. The light does not subjugate anyone by force; God does not violate anyone who refuses to retain his art. Those who are separated from the light of the Father and have transgressed the law of liberty have fallen away by their own fault, since they have been made free and masters of their decisions. And God, who knows all things beforehand, has prepared for both appropriate dwelling places: for those who seek the light of incorruptibility and hasten towards it he bountifully gives the light which they desire; for others who despise it and turn away from it and in a manner blind themselves, he has prepared darkness appropriate to the opponents of light. Now submission to God is eternal rest, so that those who fly from the light may have a place worthy of their flight and those who fly from eternal rest may also have a place worthy of their flight. For since all good things are with God, those who of their own free will fly from God defraud themselves of all good things: and being defrauded of all that is good in God's sight, they will of course fall into God's just judgment. Because those who fly from rest will justly have their conversation in punishment, and those who have fled from the light shall justly dwell in darkness. But as in this transitory light those who shrink from it enslave themselves to darkness and dwell in the dark, and the light is not the cause of their dwelling thus, similarly those who flee from the eternal light of God which contains all that is good are themselves the cause of their dwelling in eternal darkness, deprived of all good: they are made themselves the cause of their dwelling thus.

Irenaeus, *Against All the Heresies*, IV, 39.2–4

The Martyrs of Lyons

In Lyons in 177 a popular riot led to the arrest of Christians, who were condemned with the approval of the same emperor Marcus Aurelius. Eusebius has preserved the letter (by Irenaeus?) which describes these events.

Letter from the Churches of Lyons and Vienne to the Churches of Asia and Phrygia
The servants of Christ dwelling in Vienne and Lyons, in Gaul, to their brethren in Asia and Phrygia who have the same faith in redemption and the same hope, peace and grace and glory from God the Father and our Lord Christ Jesus.

To all questions Sanctus replied in Latin, 'I am a Christian.' He confessed this repeatedly as his name and city and race and everything, and the heathen did not hear anything else from him . . . Finally, when they had nothing more that they could do to him, at the last they applied red-hot brazen plates to the most tender parts of his body. His flesh was burned, but he himself continued unbent and unyielding, firm in his confession, bedewed and strengthened by the heavenly foundation of the water of life issuing from the breast of Christ. His poor body became the witness to his sufferings, for it was nothing but wound and hurt, so lacerated that it had lost the outward form of humanity. But it was Christ who suffered in him and did great wonders, destroying the enemy, and showing as a pattern to the rest that there is nothing terrible where there is the love of the Father, nothing painful where there is the glory of Christ.

Some days later they tortured the martyr again and thought that since his body was swollen and inflamed, if they applied the same torments they would overcome him, because he could not bear even a touch of the hand, or that by dying under torture he would frighten the rest. But nothing of the sort happened in his case. Moreover, beyond all human imagining his poor body revived and was restored in the later trial and recovered its former appearance and the use of the limbs, so that through the grace of Christ the second torture became not a torment but a cure.

Others had been so cruelly tortured that it did not seem as if they could live any longer even if every attention were given them. They lingered on in prison, destitute of all human care but confirmed by the Lord, and strengthened in body and soul, encouraging and consoling the rest. Others, young and arrested more recently, whose bodies had not been already inured to torture, were unable to bear the burden of confinement and died there.

Blessed Pothinus, who had been entrusted with the charge of the bishopric in Lyons, being over ninety years of age and very sick in body, scarcely breathing from his sickness but strengthened by zeal of the spirit from his vehement desire for martyrdom, was dragged on to the tribunal with the others, his body fainting with old age and disease. But his soul held up within him, thus ensuring the triumph of Christ. He was conveyed by the soldiers on to the tribunal, accompanied by the magistrates of the city and a tumultuous mob, as though he were Christ in person. His witness was sublime. When the governor asked him who was the God of the Christians, he answered, 'If you are worthy, you shall know.' . . .

Blandina was exposed hung on a stake to be the food of the beasts let loose on her. The sight of this woman, as it were crucified, praying with a loud voice, put much heart in the combatants. Their sister showed to their fleshly eyes him who was crucified for them, assuring those who believed on him that everyone who suffers for the glory of Christ has fellowship with the living God for ever . . .

Last of all the blessed Blandina, like a noble mother who has encouraged her children and sent them before her crowned with victory to the king, also herself retracing all her children's battles, hastened towards them, rejoicing and triumphing in her departure as though she was invited to a marriage supper rather than being cast to the beasts. After the whips, after the beasts, after the iron chair, she was thrown at last into a net and cast before a bull. And after being tossed for a long time by the beast, having no further sense of what was happening because of her hope and hold on the things that she had believed, and because of her communing with Christ, she herself had her throat cut, and the heathen confessed that they had never known a woman endure so many and so great sufferings . . .

Letter from the churches of Lyons and Vienne, 20, 24, 28, 29, 41, 55

A Gnostic System

The teaching of Basilides (Alexandrian Gnosticism), described by Irenaeus

According to him [Basilides], from the unborn Father is born first Mind, then from the Mind the Logos, then from the Logos Prudence, then from Prudence Wisdom and Power, and from Wisdom and Power the Virtues and Princes and Angels whom they call first, and by whom the first heaven was made. And afterwards, by emanation from these, other angels also came into existence and made a second heaven like the first. In the same manner, yet other angels . . . made a third heaven. Then, from this third series of angels a fourth emerged through degradation, and so on. In this way, they affirm, successive series of Archons and Angels came into existence, and up to 365 heavens. And this is why the year has so many days, according to the number of the heavens.

The angels who occupy the lower heaven, the heaven that we see, made all things which are in the world, and divided among themselves the earth and the nations upon it. Their chief is the one who passes as the God of the Jews. And because he wanted to subjugate the other nations to his own people, i.e. to the Jews, the other Archons stood and acted against him. For this reason, too, the other nations took a stand against his. Then the unborn and unnameable Father, seeing the perversion of the Archons, sent Mind, his firstborn son – he is the one who is called the Christ – to liberate from the domination of the authors of the world those who believed in him. He appeared to the nations of the Archons, on earth, in the form of a man, and performed mighty works. Accordingly, he himself did not suffer the passion, but a certain Simon of Cyrene was called on to bear the cross in his place. And it was Simon who was crucified, in error and ignorance . . .

So those who 'know' that have been delivered from the Archons who are authors of the world. And we should not confess him who has been crucified, but him who came in human form, seemed to be crucified, was called Jesus and was sent by the Father to destroy, through this 'economy', the works of the authors of the world. So, Basilides says, if anyone confesses the crucified one that person is still a slave and under the dominion of those who made our bodies; but he who denies him is free from their grasp and knows the 'economy' of the unborn Father.

Moreover there is salvation only for the soul, since the body is by nature corruptible.

Irenaeus, *Against All the Heresies*, I.24.3–5

The Canon of the Scriptures

Canon is a Greek word meaning 'rule'. The canon of the scriptures is the catalogue of the books recognized by the church as the rule of its faith. This is not to be confused with authenticity. The fragment of the Muratorian Canon (named after L. A. Muratori who discovered it in 1740) copies a text which goes back to the second century. It includes all the present books of the New Testament except for Hebrews, James, I & II Peter. The Shepherd is mentioned in it as a 'useful' book.

In 369 Athanasius had already compiled a list of the books of the Old and New Testaments as they now are. So did the Council of Rome in 382. Codex Sinaiticus of the fourth century, copying a second- or third-century model, contains all the present books of the New Testament.

The Interpretation of Scripture

In line with the New Testament the Fathers, without schematizing, distinguish sometimes three, sometimes four senses of scripture. The fourth sense came to be important particularly in the Middle Ages.

Three senses (Origen, Jerome)

A literal or historical sense, a spiritual or moral sense, an allegorical or typological (christological) sense. Thus the Crossing of the Red Sea is a historical event, prefiguring the saving work of Jesus, which is realized for the church and for the Christian in baptism.

Four senses (Augustine, John Cassian, Bede)

A literal, allegorical, tropological (moral) and angogical (spiritual) sense. Thus Nineveh, according to Richard of St Victor, is an Assyrian city (literal meaning), the world (allegorical meaning), the church (mystical meaning) and the soul (moral meaning).

Muratorian Canon

Named after the scholar who discovered it in Milan in the eighteenth century. It dates from the middle of the second century.

. . . but at some he (Mark) was present and so he set them down.

The third book of the Gospel is that according to Luke. This was Luke the physician whom after Christ's ascension Paul had taken with him because he enjoyed travelling. He wrote in his own name and in order, but he had not seen the Lord in the flesh either. Following the information he had been able to obtain, he began his narrative with the birth of John.

The fourth of the Gospels is by John, one of the disciples. When his fellow-disciples and bishops exhorted him (to write), he said: 'Fast with me for three days, and let us tell one another what may be revealed to any of us.' That same night it was revealed to Andrew, one of the apostles, that John was to write all things in his own name, and that the others were to examine his work.

The Acts of all the Apostles were written in one book. Luke declares to the most excellent Theophilus that everything took place in his presence, as he also plainly shows by leaving out the passion of Peter, and also the departure of Paul from Rome on his journey to Spain.

The Epistles of Paul themselves make plain to those who wish to understand it what epistles were sent by him, and from what place for what cause. Paul first wrote at some length to the Corinthians, forbidding heresies and schisms, and then to the Galatians, forbidding circumcision. Then he wrote to the Romans at greater length to show them the order of the scriptures, and to make them see that Christ is the first principle of them. It is not necessary for us to discourse on each one in detail. For the blessed apostle Paul, following the traces of John his predecessor, writes only by name to seven churches in this order: first to the Corinthians, secondly to the Ephesians, thirdly to the Philippians, fourthly to the Colossians, fifthly to the Galatians, sixthly to the Thessalonians, seventhly to the Romans. Moreover he wrote a second time to the Corinthians and the Thessalonians, to admonish them. However, it must be recognized that there is only one church spread all over the world. For John, too, in the Apocalypse, though he writes to seven churches, speaks to all. The letter to Philemon, that to Titus and the two to Timothy, although they were set down out of love (for these persons), are no less in honour of the Catholic church and for the organization of church discipline. There is also in circulation a letter to the Laodicenes, another to the Alexandrians, both fabricated in the name of Paul to suit the heresy of Marcion, and several others which cannot be received into the Catholic church, since it is not fitting for gall to be mixed with honey.

CHART OF THE FIRST THREE CENTURIES

Political events		Church history	Eastern writers	Western writers
Death of Domitian Nerva emperor Antonine dynasty, 96–192 Trajan emperor	about 95 98	John's exile on Patmos		Letter of Clement
Pliny the Younger, legate in Bithynia	about 100 111	John's death	Letters of Ignatius	
Trajan's Eastern campaign Antoninus emperor Jewish revolt Marcus Aurelius emperor Parthian invasion	116 155 161		Didache (?)	Shepherd of Hermas 156– Letter of Polycarp Justin in Rome
	161/169	Martyrdom of Polycarp of Smyrna	Letter to Diognetus	
	163/167 about 170	Martyrdom of Justin in Rome Beginnings of Montanism Irenaeus Bishop of Lyons	Papias, Bishop of Hierapolis	
Commodus joint emperor	177 179	Abgar IX, King of Edessa, first Christian ruler (?)	Melito, Bishop of Sardes Theophilus in Antioch	
Death of Marcus Aurelius Commodus sole emperor	180			Irenaeus, *Against All the Heresies*
	185 189/190	Paschal dispute under Pope Victor	Birth of Origen	
Assassination of Commodus Septimus Severus sole emperor (Dynasty of Severus 193–235)	193 194 197 197	Edict of Severus forbidding Jewish & Christian proselytism	Clement of Alexandria	Tertullian, *Apologeticum* Hippolytus in Rome
Caracalla emperor	203 207/208 211 217/222	Calixtus Pope Reform of penance Condemnation of Sabellius Schism of Hippolytus	Death of Clement	Tertullian, Montanist
Maximin emperor	235 249/250	Pope Pontian and Hippolytus deported to Sardinia Decian edict of persecution Martyrdom of Pope Fabian		
Invasion of the Goths	250 251	Cornelius Pope. Synod of Rome against the Novatian schism		
Valerian emperor The Persians capture Antioch	253 256 257/258	Synod of Carthage Persecution Martyrdom of Pope Sixtus II, and of the deacon St Laurence	Martyrdom of Origen	Martyrdom of Cyprian

2

The Church of the Martyrs
(Third Century)

A century and a half after Paul set out on his missionary journey a golden age of the church fathers began. During the third century the church spread eastwards as far as Cappadocia and Mesopotamia; it consolidated its position in Egypt, in Roman Africa, in Gaul and in Germania.

In order to give a better welcome to the influx of candidates, the church had to adapt. A three-stage hierarchy developed; in it the association between bishop and deacon remained basic, but the presbyterate took an increasingly prominent place. From now on the catechumenate lasted for three years. The preaching and activity of Origen and Cyprian aimed at a deepening of the faith. Two legislative texts appeared, though they had no official character. These were the liturgical treatise the *Apostolic Tradition* (in Rome) and the *Didascalia of the Twelve Apostles* (in the East).

For Christians, periods of calm alternated with persecutions. Christianity was sufficiently vigorous to bear the shocks. Dead leaves might fall, but the pruned tree put forth its branches. Tertullian could even say with some verve: 'Your most refined cruelties are to no purpose. We become more numerous each time you reap: the blood of Christians is a seed' (*Apologeticum* 50, 13).

From the third century onwards the church produced writers of exceptional quality: Tertullian in Carthage and Origen in Alexandria. Their actions and influence lasted long. They forged Christian language and its vocabulary, theology and exegesis, which were to nurture the Christian centuries to come.

An engraving from the Catacomb of Priscilla

An epitaph from the Christian museum in the Vatican

Hippolytus of Rome: Apostolic Tradition

We give you thanks, O God,
through your beloved Son, Jesus Christ,
that in these last times,
you sent him to us as saviour and redeemer and messenger of your will,
who is the Word inseparable, through whom you have created all things,
and on whom you have rested your favours.
You sent him from heaven into a virgin's womb,
and being conceived he became incarnate within her.
He was manifested as being your Son, born of the Holy Spirit and
   a virgin.
He fulfilled your will, making us a holy people.
He stretched forth his hands, when he suffered
to deliver from suffering those who believed in you.

Who when he was betrayed, took bread and, giving thanks, said:
Take, eat. This is my body broken for you.
Likewise also the cup, saying:
This is my blood, shed for you.

When you do this, you do it in memory of me.
Thus remembering his death and his resurrection,
We offer you the bread and cup,
giving you thanks that you have found us worthy to stand before you and serve
   you.
We ask you to send your Spirit on the offering of the holy church,
to gather into one all those who make this communion, to confirm their faith in
   truth,

That we may praise you and glorify you through your son Jesus Christ,
   to you be glory and honour
to the Father and to the Son with the Holy Spirit,
in the holy church now and for ever and world without end. Amen.

I · The Epic of Blood

In the third century, the consolidation of Christianity coincided with the weakening of the Roman empire, whose structure was crumbling (the Barbarians were at the frontiers, there was galloping inflation and a decrease in the population). The emperors, seeing that the élites, who had become Christians, lacked patriotic fervour, sought to mobilize the people through emperor worship.

Septimus Severus (193–211) wanted to halt the expansion of religious groups and forbid proselytism. The catechumenate was therefore made illegal. It was in this climate that Tertullian wrote his *To the Martyrs*. Scores of Christians who were still catechumens, among them Felicitas and Perpetua in Carthage, were arrested in 203 and died the death of martyrs.

After an interval Maximin the Thracian (235–238), who believed himself immortal because of his huge stature, promulgated an edict which ordered the 'sole heads of the churches' to be put to death. This resulted in the banishment in 235 of Pontian, Bishop of Rome, and Hippolytus, a learned scholar, to Sardinia, where they eventually died. The *Apostolic Tradition* is generally attributed to Hippolytus.

The church then experienced another respite. The emperor Decius (249–251), who was being threatened on the frontiers, wanted to assure himself of everyone's loyalty and demanded a general *supplicatio* (act of worship) for the salvation of the empire. All the citizens had to make a sacrifice to the gods, after which they received a certificate (*libellus*). Because it was so unexpected, the persecution caused a rout and resulted in the apostasy of a great many Christians. The church had a wealth of new martyrs: the priest Pionius and his companions at Smyrna, Maximus at Ephesus, Lucian and Marcian at Nicodemia, Apollinus with many others at Alexandria. We know about all these martyrs through authentic and contemporary records. On this occasion Cyprian supported the confessors in prison by his letters.

In the wake of the tornado came the problem of how to treat those who had offered sacrifices. A moderate position, advocated and put into practice by Rome and Carthage (forgiveness after an appropriate penance) clashed with the intransigent position of the rigorists.

To begin with, the reign of Valerian (253–260) was one of the most favourable towards Christians. Then great financial difficulties arose and the powers sought to use anti-Christian feeling to 'refloat the treasury'. A first edict (257) ordered the chief clergy to make sacrifices: Cyprian in Carthage and Dionysius in Alexandria were called on to obey. When they refused, they were deported. A second edict proclaimed the death penalty on those who refused. The number of martyrs increased, as did the accounts we have of them.

In Rome, Bishop Sixtus II was executed along with four of his deacons (of whom Laurence was one). Cyprian in Carthage suffered the same fate. In 258, Fructuosus was put to death at Tarragon, along with two of his deacons. We still have the accounts of the martyrdoms of Cyprian, Fructuosus and Montanus of Carthage.

The cult of martyrs has been in existence since the second century, as the history of Polycarp bears witness. It developed in the third century with the growing number of martyrs. On their anniversaries, the Acts of these illustrious confessors, which had been carefully kept in the churches, were read out: the passions of Christians like Polycarp, Felicitas and Perpetua were described by contemporary witnesses. At a later period, the legends of the martyrs were to mix up truth and fantasy; some of them are pure works of fiction, like the story of St Cecilia: all we really know is her name and that she was martyred.

In the amphitheatre, Felix, one of the brothers, went up to Fructuosus and asked him to remember him. 'I must think of the whole Catholic church, extending from the East to the West.'

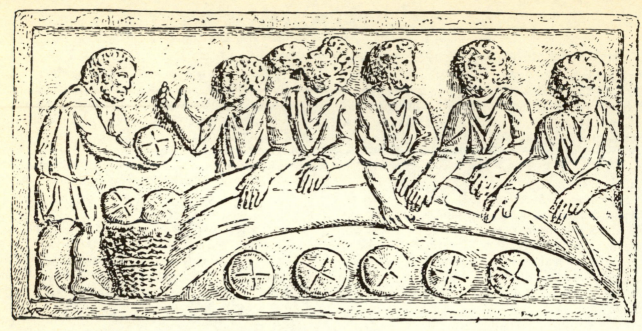

Sarcophagus from the Lateran
museum
(after O. Marucchi, *I monumenti
del museo Pio-Lateranense*,
plate XXVII.2)

Tombstone of St Perpetua

Felicitas and Perpetua, Ravenna
(photograph Roger-Viollet)

Fragment of a sarcophagus
(after Marucchi, *I monumenti*,
plate I.2)

II · Christian Thought in Alexandria

The tourist who disembarks today at the port of Alexandria gains scarcely any idea of its importance as the metropolis of Egypt, the second city of the empire, the economic and commercial trading centre of Africa and Asia, whose inhabitants used to number a million. Inheriting the position of ancient Athens, this city at the crossroads was the most active centre of Greek intellect, where all the philosophies and all the religions met.

The Museum, a replica of the hill of the Muses in Athens and originally part of Ptolemy's palace, brought together scholars and philosophers and had become a university, with the most prodigious library in the world (700,000 volumes). It fell victim to fire during the siege laid by Julius Caesar. The cultivation of papyrus, a plant which flourishes in the Nile valley, facilitated the book industry.

The Jewish community, which was particularly numerous, enjoyed important privileges and an autonomous administration. In order to make contact with the Hellenistic world easier, the rabbis of Alexandria had the audacity to translate the Hebrew Bible into Greek. Legend has it that seventy scholars were involved (hence the name Septuagint, Greek for seventy), a name which stuck to the Greek version, which was established between 250 and 150 BC. This was the version which St Paul used.

In Alexandria, too, Philo, an educated Jew, a contemporary of Christ, wrote allegorical commentaries chiefly on Genesis with the intention of pointing out the similarities between scripture and Greek philosophy. This method established a school of Christian writers of Alexandria.

Alexandria was evangelized early on (papyrus fragments of the four evangelists from the beginning of the second century are in existence), perhaps by the evangelist Mark (see Eusebius, *Church History* II, 16); later, the official church was overwhelmed by a wave of recruits from Gnosticism (Valentinus, Basilides, Carpocrates, 120/130), which imperilled the deposit of faith. The church had to wait a generation before it found men capable of arguing back against the Gnostics.

About 180 Pantaenus, a converted philosopher of Sicilian origin, became an elder of the city and head of the Catechetical School. He was to be Clement's teacher.

1. Clement of Alexandria (died about 215)

Of Greek and pagan origin, Titus Flavius Clemens had a solid education before his conversion. He set out to travel, in search of masters, and finally settled down in Alexandria.

Around 180 he entered the school of Pantaenus, who, 'plundering the grasslands of the prophets and apostles, caused a pure gnosis to be born in the souls of those who heard him' (*Stromateis* 1, 11, 1). This indicates a grasp of Christianity which both reflected and conformed to the deposit of faith.

The disciple succeeded his master as head of the Christian Didaskalia (a private school) which welcomed the educated class of the city. He did his utmost to reconcile culture and the gospel. He taught there until the persecution under Septimus Severus (202/203), when he took refuge first in Cappadocia and then in Jerusalem, where he continued to serve the church and compose his works.

As far as we know Clement was not a priest but, like Justin, a layman in the church, and worked out a Christian humanism. His works correspond to the three stages of conversion: the *Protrepticon*, the *Paedagogos* and the *Stromateis*.

The *Protrepticon* to the Greeks

The *Protrepticon* (from the Greek = turn towards) is an invitation, corresponding to a known literary genre, an appeal to heathens to 'listen to the new song of the Logos of God'. It was composed methodically, and the language is polished and enthusiastic.

An engraving from Ptolemy's
Geography

Clement speaks of paganism as one who knows it from the inside. Without emphasizing them, he brings into relief the absurdities and the impiety of the mysteries of religion and pagan myths whose weaknesses he had experienced. His aim was to lead the questioner to an encounter with the Christian God.

The work is composed like a symphony. It opens with a hymn to Christ, a theme taken up again at the end, when the author invites the whole of humankind to put itself under the direction of the Saving Word and exclaim, 'Hail, Light!' (borrowed from Aeschylus). See the extract on p. 37.

The *Paedagogos*

If the *Protrepticon* was a work for those on the threshold, the *Paedagogos* is the Christian's catechism. The Word of God became man to educate, that is to say both to instruct and mould, mankind: 'My children, we need instruction, and the whole of the human race needs Jesus' (*Paedagogos*, 1, 83.3).

Clement describes the radical change which allows us to be born anew to a different form of life and to fashion ourselves on the example of Christ the Logos, our guest dwelling within, on whom we ought to model ourselves daily in our everyday life, in our marriage and in our social dealings (prayer, meals, possessions, refusal of luxuries). All this imposes an asceticism on worldly people but allows them to radiate the gospel.

The *Stromateis*

The 8 books of the *Stromateis* (a carpet of mixed or rainbow-coloured pieces) make up the longest Christian writing composed up to that time. It is a collection of course notes on extremely varied subjects: the relationship between philosophy and revelation (I), problems of faith and of the purpose of human life (II), Christian marriage (III), martyrdom and perfection (IV), knowledge of God (V), philosophy, human knowledge, revelation (VI), the perfect Gnostic (VII), various outlines (VIII).

What rich man can be saved?

In a wealthy city like Alexandria, riches were a problem. In his commentary on the text of Mark 10.17–31, Clement explained that it is not the rich man but the unrepentant sinner who is excluded from the kingdom of God.

Doctrine and meaning

Clement comes in the wake of Justin, and has an openness towards Greek thought. To him it seemed like a foundation course, encouraging one to seek and receive the Word of God. He presents Christianity 'with a feeling of superiority and quiet assurance' (Lietzmann).

The Word of God is truly at the centre of history. His educative action begins with philosophy for the pagans and with philosophy and with the law and the prophets for the Jews. When he became incarnate, he brought this long preparation to fruition fully and perfectly. He is therefore the teacher to whom the Father entrusts humanity, so that he may reveal the truth to them. 'The one who does not know seeks; having sought, he finds the master; having found him, he believes; having believed, he hopes, and, being loved, he identifies himself with the one whom he loves, ardently desiring to be the one whom he loved before' (*Stromateis* V.17.1).

Baptismal grace and gnosis cause faith to ripen in love, by the action of God who dwells in the true believer and 'makes his life into one long celebration'.

The New Song

'In the beginning was the Word.' Thus inasmuch as the Word was from the first, he was and is the divine beginning of all things; but inasmuch as he has now assumed the name Christ, consecrated of old and worthy and powerful, I call him the New Song. At all events, the Logos, the Christ, is the cause of our being at first (for he was in God) and of our well-being. This Logos has now appeared as man, he alone being both, both God and man, and the author of all good things for us. Having been taught by him now to live well, we are introduced to eternal life. For according to that inspired apostle of the Lord, 'the grace of God which brings salvation has appeared to all men, teaching us to renounce ungodliness and worldly lust and to live soberly, righteously and godly in this present world, looking for the blessed hope and appearing of the glory of the great God and our saviour Jesus Christ'.

This is the New Song, the manifestation of the Word which was in the beginning and before the beginning. For the pre-existent Saviour recently appeared among us; he who is in him that truly is, has appeared; the Word 'who was with God' and by whom all things were created has appeared. As demiurge he gave life at the beginning as he created it; then, having appeared as a teacher, he taught us how to live in order to obtain, as God, eternal life. But now is not the first time that he took pity on us for our error; he did so from the beginning. Yet only today has he appeared to save us from our loss. For that wicked reptile, by his charlatanism, even now reduces men to slavery and maltreats them, torturing them almost like those barbarians who are said to bind their prisoners to corpses until they rot together. This wicked tyrant and dragon, having bound fast with the miserable chain of superstition all those whom he can drag to him from their birth, to stones, to pieces of wood, to images and idols of the same kind, may truly be said to have taken and buried living men with those dead idols, till both suffer corruption together.

Clement of Alexandria, *Protrepticon*, 1

Origen (Hulton Deutsch)

2. Origen (died 254): scripture, the body of the Word

There is scarcely any ancient writer about whom we are better informed than Origen, thanks to Eusebius' *History*. Born in Alexandria in about 185 in a deeply Christian family, he received a sound upbringing, both religious and secular, which he completed later at the school of the philosopher Ammonius Saccas, the teacher of Plotinus.

Leonidas, Origen's father, died a martyr's death in 202. This meant that his son, the oldest of seven children, had to provide for the family. He taught grammar, that is to say literature, with great success. Later on, Bishop Demetrius entrusted the education of catechumens to him. He led an ascetic life, selling his secular books and voluntarily making himself 'a eunuch for the kingdom of God'.

The school was brim full of pagans and Gnostics, attracted by the reputation of its young master. Origen kept the most advanced stage of teaching for himself. He put his pupils through a cycle of classical studies, ending up with systematic study of the Bible and of theology. Between 215 and 220, at the request of Ambrose, a convert from Gnosticism, he began to write his book *De Principiis* (*On Principles*).

During this period Origen travelled a great deal: to Rome, in Jordan, then to Caesarea in Palestine. He preached there, and since he was a layman, this brought the wrath of his bishop down on him.

The Bishop of Caesarea ordained Origen priest, to justify his preaching to the church. On his return to Alexandria, Demetrius banished him and deprived him of his priesthood. So Origen took refuge in Caesarea, where he founded a school similar to the one in Alexandria. He carried on with his double task of preaching and producing exegesis. When called upon for consultation he travelled to Greece and Arabia. In 250, at the time of the Decian persecution, he was thrown into prison and tortured. He died at the age of 69, about 254.

His work

Origen's output was enormous, undoubtedly the largest in Christian antiquity. The catalogue drawn up by Eusebius lists two thousand writings, of which only a fraction have come down to us. These touch on many different subjects: theology and the spiritual life: *Exhoration to Martyrdom* and *On Prayer*; controversies: *Against Celsus* (refuting the work of a pagan philosopher); but above all Holy Scripture: *Commentaries* (a verse-by-verse scholarly explanation), *Scholia* (note on difficult passages), *Homilies* (sermons to the people passed on by scribes). Finally, came the Hexapla, with the text of the Bible set out in six columns.

1	2	3	4	5	6
Hebrew text Hebrew letters	Hebrew Greek characters	Aquila translation (second century BC)	Symmachus translation (second century BC)	Septuagint translation (third-second century)	Theodotion translation (first century BC)

In the fifth and most important column, with the help of critical symbols Origen shows variants from the Hebrew and gaps – documentation on the Greek text which had never been collected before. Doubtless there was only one copy (kept in Caesarea); Jerome was still able to consult it, to his advantage, but it is now lost.

The endemic attacks on Origenism and the condemnation of theses imputed to Origen which took place at the Second Council of Constantinople in 553 resulted in the systematic destruction of his enormous output. All that remains to us is the Greek text of several of his books (*On Principles*, *Against Celsus*) and a Latin translation of others. No complete commentary has survived. A papyrus from Toura, in Egypt, discovered in 1941, has restored to us, amongst other things, the *Conversation with Heraclides*.

A Meditation by Origen

On a text of St John (reminiscent of Pascal:
'Christ is in agony until the end of the world')

If we have understood the intoxication of the saints and how it is promised to them for their joy, let us now see how our Saviour drinks no more wine until he drinks this new wine with the saints in the kingdom of God.

Now my Saviour is still afflicted by my sins. My saviour cannot be joyful as long as I remain in iniquity. Why not? Because he is the 'advocate for our sins before the Father', as his close disciple John tells us, saying that, 'if anyone has sinned, we have an advocate with the Father, Jesus Christ who is without sin, and he himself is the propitiation for our sins.' So how could he drink the wine of gladness, he who is advocate for our sins, while I sadden him by sinning? How could he be joyful, he who approaches the altar as propitiation for me, a sinner, he in whose heart sadness for my sins constantly wells up? 'I shall drink this wine with you', he says, 'in my Father's kingdom.' As long as we do not act in such a way as to ascend to the kingdom, he who has promised to drink this wine with us cannot drink it alone. So he remains in sadness as long as we persist in going astray. If his apostle 'weeps for some who have sinned and have not repented of their crimes', what do we say of our Saviour himself, who is called the son of love, who was killed for the love he had for us; who did not seek his advantage when he was equal with God but sought ours, and therefore emptied himself of himself? So having thus sought our good, now would he not seek us more now? Would he not be more concerned for our interests? Would he not suffer more when we go astray? Would he not weep more over our loss, he who wept over Jerusalem and said to it: 'How many times have I wanted to gather your children, as a hen gathers its chicks, and you would not?' Will he who has borne our hurts and has suffered for us as the physician of our souls and bodies now neglect the corruption of our wounds? . . . So for us all he stands before the face of God interceding for us; he stands by the altar, offering to God propitiation on our behalf. He waits for us to be converted, to imitate his example, to follow his footsteps, to rejoice with us and 'drink the wine with us in his father's kingdom'.

Origen, *Homily VII on Leviticus*

Teaching

Origen was the heir to Greek thought. He followed in the wake of a double tradition – Christian and Jewish – made famous by Philo, Pantaenus and Clement. He was at one and the same time a speculative theologian, a controversialist, an exegete and a spiritual writer. In different areas, he made it his business to pioneer and promote theological and exegetical research for the following centuries, in both the East and West.

The first concern of the exegete was to establish the text and then to study it in a spirit at once scientific and spiritual. Origen distinguishes three meanings in the text:

– *literal*: the meaning of a word, of a historical action, of an institution.

– *psychological*: a psychological or moral meaning, applied to the spiritual life.

– *spiritual*: allegorical or mystical meaning, opening up the mysteries of the kingdom.

Ordinarily, Origen reduces the three meanings to two: literal and spiritual. The letter is indispensable, serving to support the text and its interpretation. It contains a hidden meaning, the meaning of the Spirit, which has inspired the text. This enables the Old Testament to be read in the light of Christ, as prophecy, and the New Testament to be read as the promise of future good.

This is a reading on two levels, which from the time of Paul characterized all ancient exegesis. The principle might be rooted in the New Testament, but Origen's application of it to the tiniest details of the text is sometimes debatable. In this way, Noah's ark becomes a picture of the church, to which the Second Letter of Peter bears witness. But Origen goes further and embarks on allegory when he affirms that the 300 cubits stand for 'the whole of spiritual creation' and the 50 cubits for 'redemption and remission'; the various rooms are the various degrees of perfection.

The theologian did pioneering work in sketching out a first *Summa Theologica* in his book *On Principles*, in four volumes: 1. God; 2. the World; 3. Mankind; 4. Holy Scripture. Admittedly, this is a youthful work in which sometimes risky hypotheses proliferate, and these did him damage posthumously.

For Origen, the economy of salvation is summed up in the triple presence of God and of Christ: in scripture, in the church and amongst the faithful. Scripture, Christ and his mystical body are governed by the same law of surpassing, which goes from the letter, the flesh, the sign to the invisible mystery; from the terrestrial history of salvation (Moses, Christ, the church) to its fulfilment in the beyond.

'Therefore you too are to look for all the signs in the Old Testament and ask yourself which truths of the New Testament they foreshadow; and in the pictures of the New Testament look to see what truths they announce for the world to come, or at least for future and past ages, when the signs are accomplished' (*Commentary on St Matthew*, 122.3).

The spiritual teacher perceived the sacrament of the presence of God in the world in scripture. With a burning joy he sought the Bride of the Song of Songs, that hidden presence which he had to discover at all costs. Beyond the letter and the form in which it was expressed he had to encounter the incarnate and crucified Christ in glory.

From now on, the mystery of the cross provided the rhythm for the march across the desert, with its hardships, stripping away the world of the senses, the victory over passions, the awakening of inner meanings, union with the Word of God. Transformation in the spirit has to be a perpetual progress. Origen describes this in three stages (which were then to be taken up by all the mystics): from purification and illumination to the nuptial union, likeness to God.

In the words of Hans Urs von Balthasar, two hundred years after Christ and two hundred years before Augustine, Origen gave Christian theology its stature.

Understanding Scripture

An example of the way in which Origen goes from the literal interpretation, referring to the rabbinic tradition, to the 'mystical' meaning, in order to reach the moral application.

Moses is ordered to strike the sea with his rod so that it divides and withdraws for the people of God to pass through, and so that this element of water which was an object of fear to them may obey the divine will, forming a wall to right and left which is not a danger but a protection. So the water is driven into a heap and the restrained water curves in on itself. The liquid becomes solid and the bottom of the sea is dry sand.

Notice the goodness of God the Creator. If you obey his will and follow his law, he compels the elements themselves to serve you even against their own nature. I have heard a tradition from the ancients that in this passage through the sea the waters divided individually for each individual tribe of the sons of Israel and a special way was made for each tribe. The proof would be what is written in the Psalms: 'He who divided the Red Sea into divisions' . . . I thought it pious not to omit this observation by the ancients on the divine scriptures.

So what teaching is given us by this? I already gave the apostle's interpretation above. He calls this 'baptism accomplished by Moses in the cloud and in the sea', that you who were baptized in Christ, in water and the Holy Spirit, might know that the Egyptians are following you and wish to recall you to your former slavery, namely among the 'rulers of this world' and the 'evil spirits' whom you previously served. These seek to catch you up, but you descend into the water and come out safe and sound; having washed away the filth of sin, you ascend 'a new man' ready to sing 'the new song' . . .

For he who does not do the works of darkness destroys the Egyptian; he who does not live carnally but spiritually destroys the Egyptian; he who either casts out of his heart all sordid and impure thoughts or does not entertain them at all destroys the Egyptian – as the apostle says, 'Take up the shield of faith to extinguish the fiery darts of the evil one.' In this way, therefore, we can see even today 'the bodies of the Egyptians stretched out on the shore', their chariots and horsemen drowned. We can even see Pharaoh in person drowned if we live by such faith that 'God may quickly grind Satan under our feet' by Jesus Christ our Lord.

Origen, *Homilies on Exodus*, V, 5

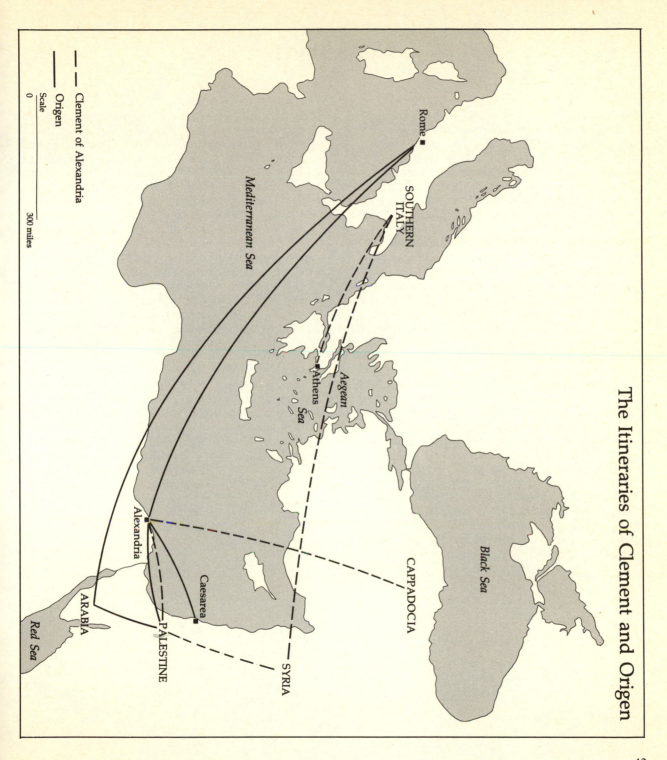

The Itineraries of Clement and Origen

God's Thirst

So the wells dug by Abraham, that is the scriptures of the Old Testament, have been filled with earth by the Philistines, who are the scribes and Pharisees, or even hostile powers. These have stopped up the openings to prevent the descendants of Abraham from drinking. Consequently people cannot drink from the scriptures, but suffer a thirst for the word of God until Isaac comes to open them so that his servants may drink.

Thanks be to Christ, the son of Abraham, of whom it is written: 'The book of the generation of Jesus Christ, the son of David, the son of Abraham.' He has come and opened up the wells for us. He opened them for those who recognized, 'Was not our heart burning in us when he opened the scriptures to us?' So he opened these wells and called them, as the text says, 'as his father Abraham had called them'. For he did not change the names of the wells.

It is astonishing that Moses is still called Moses among us; each of the prophets is addressed by his own name. For Christ did not change the names in them, but the interpretation. The change that he brought about consists in diverting us from 'Jewish fables' and 'endless genealogies', for it is written: 'They turn away from the truth and are turned to fables.'

Christ has opened the wells to us and has taught us not to seek God in a particular place but to know that 'sacrifice is offered to his name in every land'. For now the time has come when the true worshippers no longer worship the Father in Jerusalem or on Mount Gerizim but 'in spirit and in truth'. For God does not dwell in a place or a land, but he dwells in the human heart. Are you seeking God's abode? He dwells in pure hearts. He announces by the prophet that he will dwell there: 'I will dwell in them and walk in them; they shall be my people and I will be their God,' says the Lord.

Consider, therefore, that in each one of us there is a well of living water; there is a kind of heavenly meaning and latent image of God. This is the well which the Philistines, i.e. the hostile powers, have filled with earth. With what kind of earth? With the desires of the flesh, with earthly thoughts. That is why 'we have borne the image of the earthly man'. It was when we were bearing the image of the earthly man that the Philistines filled in our wells.

But now our Isaac has come, so let us welcome him and dig out our wells, casting all the earth from them. Let us purge them of all filth, of all muddy and earthly thoughts. Then we shall see springing up in them the living water of which the Lord affirms that 'He who believes in me, rivers of living water shall flow from within him.' Consider the generosity of God: the Philistines filled in our wells and blocked our small and trifling conduits of water; and in place of these springs and rivers are restored to us.

Origen, *Homilies on Genesis*, 13, 1

III · Living as a Christian in North Africa

The gospel will have reached Africa with cargo coming from the Levant. Converted Libyans are mentioned among the Jews gathered at Jerusalem. Now Libya was part of the Roman empire. Tertullian and later Augustine stated that their church was Eastern in origin. The first converts will have come from the Jewish community. Excavations at Hadrumeta have uncovered Christian tombs in the Jewish cemetery which could date from 50/60.

This is a silent church, the first document from which is the *Acts of the Martyrs of Scilli*, a small town which has never been identified. It is written in Latin. Brought before the proconsul of Carthage, these Christians were condemned 'to perish by the sword' on 17 July 180. So the gospel had penetrated the interior and reached the countryside governed by the proconsul.

The martyrs of Scilli knew and used a Latin translation of the letters of St Paul which one of them carried in a *capsa* (box). The acts of their martyrdom are the first Latin Christian text and are as it were the pride of African Christianity. Tertullian alludes to them (*To Scapula*, 3).

The first African Christian writers whom we shall meet are different from those of Alexandria. Although African, they are marked by a Latin genius and by Roman law. They resort to legal rather than philosophical vocabulary to forge a theological language. More pragmatic than speculative, Tertullian and Cyprian give priority to pastoral work and ethics.

1. Tertullian, or God's corsair (c. 155–212)

Life

Quintus Septimius Florens Tertullianus was the son of a centurion, the highest rank that a non-Roman could attain. He bears the stamp of it: rigour and a predilection for the word discipline. The young African received a solid education, studying law and rhetoric. He perhaps worked as an advo-cate in Rome, and then returned to Africa, which was in his blood.

Struck by the morals of Christians, which were at the opposite extreme to paganism, Tertullian was converted after a stormy youth. To the young community, already strong in numbers and organized hierarchically, he was to bring the zeal of a new convert, the verve of his genius and the intransigence of a temperament which went to extremes. He is a cross between Tacitus and African baroque.

Work

His work is mainly polemical, apologetic and ascetical.

The apologist writes in a climate of confrontation with the Roman authorities in the time of Septimus Severus, who was concerned to impose his authority on the imperial cult (193–211). Africa was to see new martyrs. Around 197 Tertullian wrote his exhortation *To the Martyrs* for the catechumens in prison. 'Even if the body is imprisoned, all is open to the spirit. The spirit is at large, it has space . . . before you opens the road which leads to God' (2.9).

Tertullian's main apologetic work is his *Apologeticum*, a vibrant plea for the Christian cause addressed to the governors of the Roman provinces. In his

---

The Martyrs of Scilli

Saturninus read out the sentence on the tablet: 'Speratus, Nartzalus, Cittinus, Donata, Vestia, Secunda and all the others have confessed to living by the Christian rite. Since they have been offered the chance to return to the Roman religion and have obstinately refused, we condemn them to perish by the sword.'

Speratus: 'We give thanks to God.'

Acts of the Martyrs of Scilli

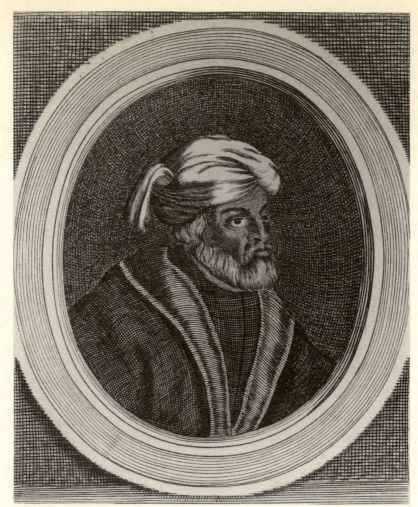

Tertullian in the year 200
(Hulton Deutsch)

Tertullian, the Creator of Christian Latin

Tertullian shaped theological vocabulary by using legal terms.

Sacramentum first of all means the depositing of a sum (a pledge) for a trial. Then it means the military oath of the recruit. Tertullian uses it for the commitment given in baptism, in the service of Christ.

Persona, which translates the Greek *hypostasis* (substance) or *prosopon* (mask, person), means mask, role, individuality, person. Tertullian uses it for the persons of the Trinity.
In numerous other cases he is happy to transliterate Greek terms, like *agape* (love), *exomologesis* (penitence) and *sphragis* (seal).

charges he denounces the irregularities of the other party, chastizes an opponent who refuses to hear what the defence has to say, and calls for freedom of religion: 'Take care that it is not already a crime of religion to take from people freedom of religion.'

The polemicist   Tertullian is a cut-and-thrust Christian and loves the fire of battle. A large number of his books are 'Against'. He writes against the Jews, the heretics, the pagans. In the wake of Irenaeus he combats the Gnostics: *Against Marcion*, *Against Hermogenes*, *Against the Valentinians*; these are followed by *The Flesh of Christ* and *The Resurrection of the Dead*. He expounds the doctrine of the Trinity in *Against Praxeas*. He finally dismisses the heretics as illegitimate innovators.

'Who are you? How long have you existed? Who gave you the right, Marcion, to put the axe to my wood? This is my land. I have in my hands the authentic title deeds, received from the very proprietors to whom the land belongs: I am the heir of the apostles.'

The master of the Christian community and of asceticism
Whether or not he was a priest, Tertullian is an outstanding member of his community, and he dazzles it, instructs it, disturbs it. Two books give us some knowledge of the life of the community: *On Baptism* and *On Prayer*. The former is a catechesis which describes biblical typology, ritual and the doctrine of the sacrament, in which as little fish we are born to the life of the Icthys (Christ) and of the Trinity.

On Prayer has delighted generations. In it Tertullian writes a commentary on the Our Father, and then outlines the conditions and characteristics of Christian prayer. Here is the preamble.

> *Of God the spirit*
> *and God the word*
> *and God the wisdom*
> *and the spirit of both:*
> *Jesus Christ our Lord ordained a new form of prayer for*
> *the new disciples of the New Testament.*

The whole book is in the same style and has the same conciseness. A married man, Tertullian was very interested in women. He wrote a book *On the Dress of Women*. He also wrote a book *To my wife*, in which he communicated to her his wishes if he should die. She should not remarry! If it is traditional to quote his fierce words about women, sometimes hardened to pleasure, Tertullian is a scrupulous and demanding moralist, even if he does praise the Christian home.

The Montanist   Finding the community too moderate, this intransigent rigorist finally succumbed to the 'Pentecostalism' of Montanus and his sect, who preached the imminent incarnation of the Holy Spirit. It is from this period that his last works date, like *On the Crown*, in which he proves to be a conscientious objector; *On Flight*, in which he rebukes those who fled during persecution; *On the Veiling of Virgins*, *An Exhortation to Chastity*, *On Monogamy*, and *On Modesty*.

Tertullian ended by founding his own sect, the Tertullianists, the last members of which were brought back to the church by Augustine.

Significance and influence

It would be difficult to overestimate the stature and genius of this baroque African. He prefers the language of law to that of philosophy for translating Christian doctrine. If need be, he creates neologisms like *agape* (love), *encrateia* (continence). He is the father of theological Latin, and he moulded trinitarian formulations in bronze.

Like Irenaeus, his vision of history allowed him to put Christ at the centre and the summit of creation and the time-line. 'All that was expressed in the mud was conceived with reference to Christ, who was to become man, namely mud, and the Word, who was to become flesh, namely earth, in his time.'

Finally, history and the Christian condition point towards fulfilment. The Alpha contains within itself the Omega which it already prophesies and for which it prepares. This is a dynamic of tension which moves both Tertullian's theology and his asceticism towards eschatology.

APOLOGYTICŪ TERTULLIANI
DEIGNORINTIA IN XPO IHŪ.

S INON LICET UOBISROMANI
imperii antistites inaperto exedito
ipso fere uerticeciuitatis praesidentabus. ad
iudicandum palam displicere. excoram exami
nare quidsit liquido incausa xpianorum
Siadhancsolam speciem, auctoritas uestra
deiustiaediligentia inpublico auramet
auterubesat inquirere. Sideniq: quodpro
xime accidit.domesticas iudiciis nimisopera
ta infestatio sectæ huius obstruit defensioni.
licet uenuit ueloculta uia tacitarum litte

Manuscript of the *Apologeticum*

Tertullian's *Apologeticum*

The introduction gives the reasons for the present plea.
People hate the Christians without knowing them.
Those who come to know Christianity hasten to join it.

Magistrates of the Roman empire, you are seated before the eyes of all, in almost the highest position in the state, to pronounce judgment. Confronted with the multitudes, you do not dare to examine the Christian cause publicly. Your authority fears and blushes to conduct a public investigation according to the most basic rules of justice. Recently you have closed your mouths to our defence, out of hatred of our 'sect', while being all too happy to receive family denunciations. At the least, give a hearing to the silent words of this writing, which brings you an expression of the truth.

Truth makes no plea on its own behalf, because truth does not wonder at its present condition. Truth knows that it plays the role of an alien on earth, and expects the hatred of those ignorant of it. Truth knows that its origin, abode, hope, recompense and honour are in heaven. And meanwhile its one desire is not to be condemned unheard.

What have your laws, which have sovereign rule in their domain, to lose in giving truth a hearing? Does their power become all the more glorious if they condemn truth without a hearing? But if they condemn truth without a hearing, they will incur the stigma of acting unjustly; in addition they will be justly suspect because, had they listened to the truth, they would not have been able to issue a condemnation.

The first grievance which we have against you is your hatred of Christianity. Your ignorance of it might seem to be an excuse, but in fact that makes it all the more unjust and criminal. For what is more unjust than to hate something that you do not know, even if that thing were hateful? One can only hate for valid reasons; otherwise hatred is blind and can only be justified by chance. And why should such hatred not in the end be completely unjusti-fied, being motivated by what it detests? So too we charge you with the foolishness of hating us out of ignorance, and with the injustice of doing it with no reason.

The proof of their ignorance, which condemns their injustice despite the excuses that might be given, is this. In the case of all those who formerly hated us without knowing us, their hatred came to an end once their ignorance ceased. There are even those who became Christians, in full knowledge of our cause; they begin to detest their past prejudices and to profess that which once they scorned. They are as numerous as you allege that we are.

So people cry out everywhere that the city is full of Christians: they are in the country, in the villages, on the islands; men and women, of every age, of every state and rank of life, are coming over to this group, and this you lament as though it were some disaster.

And in spite of that, it would never occur to you that there is a hidden treasure here. People are never concerned to verify this hypothesis; they never wish to try it out. All the others let their curiosity slumber; they delight in their ignorance, while others rejoice in their knowledge. How much more fault would Anacharsis have found with those without knowledge who pass judgment on those with knowledge?

They prefer to remain ignorant because they are already full of hatred, since knowledge of Christianity would prevent them from hating it. In fact, if there is no legitimate cause for hatred, it is better to renounce an unjust hatred. If, by contrast, one becomes convinced that hatred is justified, it does not grow any the less but becomes intensified. That is a further reason for persevering in it, along with the satisfaction of being right.

Tertullian, *Apologeticum* 1

plague. During the first persecution he hid not far from the city, continuing to direct, encourage and exhort his crippled community.

On his return, he tackled the problem of the apostates, agreeing with Rome in adopting a moderate solution. Here he had to face dissidents, led by Felicissimus. He regularly convened biennial councils at Carthage to deal with major problems. He was the primate of Africa. In opposition to Rome, along with the other bishops he declared the baptism of heretics invalid. In 257 he was arrested; first he was sent into exile, but later he was condemned to death and beheaded on 16 September 258. His life ran its course like a liturgy. He became the most famous of the African martyrs (see p. 51).

2. Governor of the Church in North Africa: Cyprian of Carthage (died 258)

Life

A generation separates Cyprian from Tertullian (as it separates Origen from Clement in the same period). Cyprian was forty at the time of his conversion, around 247. From a pagan family with a good background, he studied literature and rhetoric. He was a celebrated orator and taught with verve.

conversion + promotion

Cyprian's reading of the Bible and the influence of the priest Cecilian seem to have been the determining factors in his conversion, which was a sensation in the city of Carthage. He describes it in *To Donatus*, which is a kind of confession. Converted, Cyprian distributed the greater part of his goods to the poor. He rapidly became a priest and then, at the beginning of 249, was elected bishop of the city, 'by the judgment of God and the suffrage of the people', despite the opposition of a number of priests.

qualities

Cyprian had all the qualities for government: clearsightedness and balance, gentleness and firmness – the qualities of a leader – a passion for the church. He vigorously devoted himself to the restoration of discipline and the reform of morals.

life + its events

His time as bishop was disrupted by the two persecutions of Decius and Valerian, and by the

The writer

Cyprian was the first bishop to write in the West. His work is an extension of his pastoral action, his catechesis and his preaching. His main interests are scripture, the unity of the church, baptism, penitence and martyrdom. If he does not have the panache of Tertullian, he avoids his excesses and shows moderation. He wrote with such elegance that people called him the Christian Cicero.

The reader of the Bible Once converted, Cyprian never let go of the Bible. He compiled two *Books to Quirinus* or *Testimonies*, a methodical dossier of biblical texts to be used in catechesis and in controversy with the Jews. This was a reading of the Old Testament in terms of Christ, the church being the true Israel. Cyprian added a third book of his own devising for the use of preachers, in which he developed biblical examples in order to mobilize Christians.

The champion of church unity Africa had been afflicted with an endemic evil, division. Cyprian, and later Augustine in the face of Donatism, did not cease to struggle against this scourge. The church was the bishop's passion. It was he who coined the famous saying 'No one can have God as Father who does not have the church as mother.' It comes from the treatise *On the Unity of the Church*, the first treatise on ecclesiology. For Cyprian, unity lies in the unity of the body of bishops, in union with the apostolic see, but the local episcopate is the concrete sign of church unity. The bishop seeks to defend African particularism against centralized authoritarianism. Cyprian also wrote a treatise *On Those who Lapsed*, aimed at a reconciliation with those who had sacrificed, or had bought a certificate to say that they had. He commended penance, the nature of which was to depend on the seriousness of the fault.

The pastoral action of the bishop Like St Paul, Cyprian extended the scope of his pastoral work by letters, of which he was careful to keep copies. Some of them are short treatises, like Letter 63 on the eucharist. Sixty-five of them have come down to us, dealing with topical questions: the Roman primacy, schism, the baptism of heretics, infant baptism and the daily life of the community of Carthage.

Finally, brief treatises are devoted to problems of church life and spiritual life: works of mercy (*On Works and Almsgiving*), non-violence and peace (*On the Good and Patience*), comfort in epidemics (*On Mortality*), the vocation of consecrated virgins (*The State of Virgins*), initiation into prayer (*The Lord's Prayer*) and the heroic example of martyrdom (*Exhortation to Martyrdom*).

Cyprian's martyrdom added to his stature as a pastor – 'one of the finest episcopal figures in the history of the church' – and his work on martyrdom was one of the most read and the most copied, and the first to be printed and translated. Cyprian is almost effortlessly great, heroic without tenseness because the hour and the need for an example require it. Only his death gave full measure to his life.

The Martyrdom of Cyprian, Bishop of Carthage, in 258

The proconsul Galerius Maximus ordered Cyprian to be brought before him . . .

Proconsul: Are you Thascius Cyprianus?

Cyprian: I am.

Proconsul: Have you allowed yourself to be called 'pope'* of persons holding sacrilegious opinions?

Cyprian: I have.

Proconsul: The most sacred emperors have ordered you to offer sacrifice.

Cyprian: I will not do it.

Proconsul: Have a care for yourself . . .

Cyprian: Do as you are bid. There is no room for discussion when the issue is so clear.

Galerius Maximus consulted with his council and with grief and regret delivered this sentence. 'You have lived for a long time holding sacrilegious opinions. You have gathered a large number of accomplices around you in your blameworthy conspiracy. You have proved an enemy to the Roman gods and their sacred worship. Nor have the pious and most sacred Emperors Valerian and Gallienus, the Augusti, and Valerian, the noble Caesar, been able to recall you to the observance of their rites. And so since you have been convicted as the instigator and ringleader in most atrocious crimes, you shall be an example to the accomplices in your crime. Your blood shall be shed in accordance with the law.'

After saying this, the proconsul read the verdict from his tablet: 'We command that Cyprianus be executed by the sword.'

Bishop Cyprian said 'Thanks be to God'.

*The word 'pope' is used for all bishops up to the fifth century. It means 'father'.

The Persecutions and Deeds of Martyrs

The persecution of Nero, attested by the historian Tacitus, in 63

First they arrested those who confessed; then, upon their information, an immense multitude was convicted, not so much of the crime of arson as of hatred of the human race. Mockery of every sort was added to their deaths. Covered with the skins of beasts, they were torn by dogs and perished, or were nailed to crosses, or set on fire to illuminate the night when daylight failed.

Nero had thrown open his gardens for the spectacle, and gave a show in the circus; there he mingled with the people in the dress of a charioteer or drove about on a chariot. Thus though these men deserved extreme and exemplary punishment, there arose a feeling of compassion, because they were being sacrificed not for the public good but to satisfy one man's cruelty.

Annals, 15, 44

Trajan's instructions to Pliny the Younger, in 111/113

You have adopted the right course, my dear Secundus, in your examination of the cases of those who were accused to you as Christians. No firm rule can be laid down for all cases in such a matter. They are not to be sought out; but if they are accused and convicted, they must be punished. However, this on condition that anyone who denies being a Christian and proves this by his actions, that is by worshipping our gods, shall obtain pardon as a reward for penitence, however suspicious his past conduct may have been. As for anonymous denunciations, these must be disregarded in any charge, since this is a very bad example and unworthy of our time.

Letters, X, 96

Justin dies a martyr's death in Rome under Marcus Aurelius, in 163

The saints were all arrested together. They were then led to the Roman prefect, Rusticus. When they had come before the tribunal, the prefect Rusticus said to Justin: 'First of all, show submission to the gods and obedience to the emperors.'

Justin: No one can be blamed or condemned for having obeyed the commandments of our saviour Jesus Christ.

Prefect Rusticus: To what science are you dedicated?

Justin: I have studied all the sciences, one after another. I have ended by becoming an adherent of the true doctrine of Christians, although this is displeasing to those who are misled by error.

Rusticus: And does this science please you, unhappy one?

Justin: Yes, because by following Christians I adhere to the true doctrine.

Rusticus: What is this doctrine?

Justin: We worship the Christian God; we believe this God to be unique, since from the very beginning he has been the creator and the demiurge of the whole universe, of everything visible and invisible. We believe that Jesus Christ, the Son of God, is Lord: announced by the prophets of old as coming to dwell among mankind, the messenger of salvation and lord of all true knowledge. I, who am only a man, am too insignificant to speak worthily of his infinite divinity; I realize that that needs the power of a prophet. But there are predictions concerning the one I speak of as the Son of God. Now the prophets were inspired from on high, when they announced his coming among mankind.

Rusticus: Where do you meet?

Justin: Where we want to and are able to. Do you believe that we meet together in a particular place? Certainly not. The God of Christians is not imprisoned in one place. He is invisible, he fills the heaven and the earth. He is worshipped and glorified by the faithful everywhere.

Perpetua and Felicitas (in 203)

Part of this document is written in Perpetua's hand, which gives it special value; rarely are testimonies written by the martyrs themselves, and rarer still by women martyrs.

After a few days there was a rumour that we were to be examined. My father arrived in haste from Thurburbo, broken with sorrow. He came up the hill to see me to break my resolve, saying, 'Daughter, pity my white hairs! Pity your father, if I am still worthy for you to call me father. With these hands I brought you up to the prime of life; I preferred you to all your brothers. Do not make me a laughing stock. Think of your brothers, think of your mother and your aunt; think of your child, who cannot live without you. Go back on your decision; do not ruin all of us, for none of us will ever speak freely again if you are condemned.'

That is what my father said in his love for me, kissing his hands and throwing himself at my feet, and with tears he no longer called me 'daughter' but 'Lady'. And I grieved to see my father in this state because he alone of all my family would not rejoice at my passion. I comforted him by saying: 'Nothing will happen on the tribunal platform except what God wills. You know very well that we are not in our own power but in the power of God.' And full of sorrow, he left me.

The day of their victory dawned, and the martyrs went from the prison to the amphitheatre as if they were on their way to heaven. Their faces were radiant; they were beautiful. They were moved, not by fear but by joy. Perpetua followed at a gentle pace, as a great lady of Christ, as the darling of God; the power of her gaze forced the spectators to lower their eyes. Felicitas followed her, rejoicing that she had given birth in safety so that she might fight the beasts, from blood to blood, from midwife to gladiator, to find in her second baptism her purification from childbirth.

On the day before the games the prisoners had their last meal, which they called 'the free meal'. As far as they could, the martyrs celebrated this meal not as a festivity but as an agape. They spoke to the crowd with their usual courage, threatening them with the judgment of God, calling to witness their happiness at giving their lives, and laughing at the inquisitiveness of the crowd.

Perpetua had time to savour pain; struck between the ribs she uttered a loud cry; then she herself guided to her throat the wavering hand of the young untried gladiator. Doubtless so great a woman, who was so feared by the demon, could not be killed except of her own choosing.

O valiant and blessed martyrs! You have been called and chosen to the glory of Jesus Christ our Lord. Those who magnify, honour and adore that glory should read these new examples for the edification of the church, because they are no less precious than those of former times. They bear witness that one and the same Spirit still acts, and bear witness to the Father, God Almighty, and his Son Jesus Christ, our Lord, to whom belong splendour and power immeasurable for ever and ever! Amen.

The Martyrdom of Perpetua and Felicitas

Cyprian describes the experience of his conversion and his baptism

As for me, while I lay prostrate in the shadows of a pitch-dark night, and was tossed to and fro on the waves of this troubled world, ignorant of my true life, a stranger to life and truth, I used to think difficult what the divine mercy promised for my salvation, given the kind of life that I led. The promise was that one could be born anew, and, being given a new life in the bath of water which brings salvation, could strip off one's natural self and thus, while keeping one's physical constitution, be changed in heart and soul.

That is what I often told myself. Indeed I too was held back, encumbered with the many sins of my former life, of which I believed that I could not rid myself. Thus I gave way to the vices which were part of me; despairing of anything better, I encouraged the evils of my heart as though they were slaves born in my house or my own offspring.

But after the stains of my former life had been washed away with the aid of the water which brings regeneration and the light from on high had poured into my cleansed and hallowed breast, after I had received the Spirit which comes from heaven and a second birth had changed me into a new man, then in a marvellous way I saw certainty remove my doubts, barriers open, the darkness lighten, that which had once seemed difficult now prove easy. I found it possible to do what I had thought impossible, and with the instruction that was given me I could recognize as earthly that which formerly, born of the flesh, was inclined to sin, and that which had been enlivened in me by the Spirit as already being divine. You surely know and recognize as I do what this death of sin and life of virtue has taken away from us or brought to us.

Cyprian, *To Donatus*, 2–3

The agreement between Cornelius and Cyprian

*Cyprian expresses his regard for Pope Cornelius
and bears witness to their profound accord in difficult circumstances*

We have received, dearest brother, the glorious testimony of your faith and courage, and your fine confession gave us so much joy that we consider ourselves to be partakers in your merits and glory. For since we have one church, one mind and heart, what bishop would not rejoice at the glory of another bishop as though it were his own, and what group of brothers would not be happy to see the joy of others? It is impossible to describe all the happiness, all the satisfaction that was shown here when we learned this glad news of your courage; when we learned that you had been a leader to the brothers in confessing, and also that the confession of the leader had been enhanced by the support of the brotherhood. So in leading the way on the march to glory, you have had many companions in glory; you have persuaded the faithful to be confessors by showing yourself prepared to go first in confessing for all. We do not know what to praise more in you, your ready and firm faith or this affection of the brotherhood which allows of no separation. The courage of the bishop leading the way has been shown publicly, and the union of the brotherhood following the bishop has similarly been affirmed. Among you there is only one heart and one voice, and all the church of Rome has confessed Jesus Christ . . .

Let each one think of the other in the union of hearts and bodies, and let each of us on either side pray for one another. In moments of persecution and difficulty let us support one another in mutual love, and if God gives one of us grace to die soon and to go before the other, let our friendship continue in the presence of the Lord; let our prayers for our brothers and sisters never cease to call on the mercy of the Father. I hope, dearest brother, that things always go well with you.

Cyprian, *Letter 60 to Cornelius*, V, 2, 4

3. Being humanist and Christian: Lactantius (died after 330)

Lactantius is a transitional figure. He was born in Africa shortly before Cyprian's martyrdom. Diocletian gave him a professorial chair in Nicomedia. Since in the meantime he had become a Christian, persecution forced him to give up his teaching. He remained in the city until Constantine called him to Trier. He died around 330.

A layman, Lactantius was above all a Christian humanist, little versed in theology. He was an apologist and a pamphleteer in his book *On the Death of the Persecutors*, in which he relates their sorry end, from 303 to 313.

His magnum opus is the *Divine Institutes*, in seven volumes. His plan is to denounce the errors of pagan religion and to make the charges of irrationality made by pagan thinkers against Catholic faith rebound against them. Here the author is dependent on Cicero. In sketching out the broad outline of the Christian revelation, Lactantius begins from ancient culture to show that Christian wisdom is its true crown.

This was certainly an ambitious project, too ambitious for this humanist, who was too inadequately prepared theologically for his enterprise to be comparable to those of the masters of the fourth century.

The Sentiment of Humanity

I have spoken about what is owed to God. Now I want to speak about what is owed to man, although what is owed to man still equally relates to God, since man is the image of God.

The first duty of justice concerns God and binds us to him; the second concerns man. The name of the first is religion; the name of the second is mercy or humanity. Religion is a characteristic of the just and those who worship God. It alone is life.

God made man naked and fragile in order to teach him wisdom. In particular he gave him this affection of piety in order that man might protect his fellow man, love him, cherish him, defend him against all dangers and give him help. The strongest bond which unites men is humanity. Anyone who breaks it is a criminal and a parricide.

We all derive our origin from the same father, so we are all of the same blood. Therefore the greatest crime is to hate man or do him harm. That is why we are forbidden to nurture enmity or to encourage it. So if we are the work of the same father, what else are we but brothers? The bond which unites our souls is therefore stronger than that which unites our bodies. So Lucretius is right in saying:

Finally, we are all spring from heavenly seed.
To all that same one is Father.

We must therefore show humanity if we want to deserve the name of human beings. And showing humanity means loving our fellow man because he is man, as we too are ourselves.

Lactantius, *The Divine Institutes*, 6.10

CHART OF THE FOURTH AND FIFTH CENTURIES

General history		Church history	Eastern authors	Western authors
Constantine master of the West	312		Eusebius Bishop of Caesarea	
	314	Synod of Arles		
	325	Council of Nicaea		
Foundation of Constantinople (330)		329 – Athanasius bishop, of Alexandria	Birth of Ambrose	
	335	Death of Arius		
Constantius sole emperor	339	Persian persecution		
Invasion by the Franks,	346	Rule of Pachomius	Cyril Bishop of Jerusalem	Hilary Bishop of Poitiers
Alamans and Saxons (355)	356	Death of Antony the Hermit		
	366	Damasus pope		
				Death of Hilary
	370		Basil Bishop of Caesarea	Death of Ephraem
				Ambrose bishop
Gratian emperor of the West (375–383) with Valentinian II (375/392)	375	Beginning of Priscillianism	Epiphanius Bishop of Salamis	
Theodosius emperor of the East (379–395)				
	381	Council of Constantinople		Jerome at Rome
	384	Siricius pope		Baptism of Augustine
Valentinian II assassinated by Arbogast (392)	390		Death of Gregory of Nazianzus	Paulinus at Nola
	393			
Death of Theodosius (395)			394 – death of Gregory the Great	Augustine Bishop of Hippo
			397 – John Chrysostom Bishop of Constantiople	
	405			Death of Prudentius
Vandals cross the Rhine	409			Vincent at Lérins
Fall of Rome	410			
Siege of Hippo by the Vandals	430			
	431	Council of Ephesus		
Genseric occupies Carthage	439	Leo pope		440–50 Prosper at Rome
	451	Council of Chalcedon		
Fall of the last Western emperor	476			496 Birth of Romanus

3
The Golden Age
(Fourth and Fifth Centuries)

The fourth century is one of the most eventful and varied centuries in the history of Christianity. It opened with a great persecution and ended with the reconciliation of the parties in conflict, Christianity and Rome. It saw the appearance of the first great theological controversies along with the renowned defenders of orthodoxy. The church which organized itself at this time experienced both extension and division.

I · From Diocletian to Constantine the Great

The Emperor Diocletian (284–305) spent the first years of his reign restoring the imperial power, reforming administration and the army, and removing foreign threats. A change of policy came about in 302 under the influence of an adventurer from Sofia, the co-regent Galerius. The powerful Dalmatian unleashed an anti-Christian offensive with radical measures: the destruction of churches, the seizure of sacred books, and a ban on religious assemblies.

This persecution, the longest in Roman history, was to last ten years. It was moderated in the West, but implacable in the East, above all in Palestine and Egypt. The list of victims is a long one. No other persecution has left us so many disturbing accounts.

When a terminal illness struck him, Galerius sought reconciliation with the God of the Christians and published an edict which put an end to the persecutions. Lactantius was able to read it on the walls of the city of Nicomedia on 10 April 311. Here was a victory of the cross and the heroism of the martyrs.

After the victory over Maxentius at the Milvian Bridge, Constantine, now master of the West, decided to favour the Christians. Having become sole ruler of both the Eastern and the Western empire when he defeated Licinius in 324, he founded Constantinople to seal their unity and sought to disseminate the Christian faith everywhere.

Between the abdication of Diocletian and the

death of Theodosius in 395 the Roman empire was united under the authority of the same person for only twenty-two years. So the common destiny was both fragile and ephemeral. The splitting of the empire into two halves, in the fourth and above all in the fifth century, was to shake the church profoundly. Greek and Latin writers inhabited two different cultural spheres and worked out their theology in terms of their own cultural background. From now on the Greek language was no longer the unifying factor. The West was Latinized.

The fathers of the fourth century represent a fulcrum between the ancient heritage, which had been completely assimilated, and a Christian thought which had come to maturity. The East was enriched by the theological contribution of Cappadocia; the Latin West asserted itself beyond the Mediterranean, in Rome, Milan, Gaul, Spain and as far as the banks of the Danube.

The interlude of the Emperor Julian, a Christian who reverted to paganism, allowed bishops to leave an exile imposed because of their loyalty to Nicaea. The imperial edict which forbade Christians 'to teach that in which they no longer believe' made the church aware of the moral line between them and pagan works, and brought to birth the idea of a teaching and culture inspired by Christianity. The works of Gregory of Nazianzus, Augustine, Paulinus and Juvencus are evidence of this.

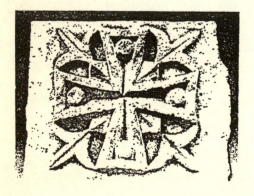

A fifth/sixth century cross

58

1. Christianity a state religion

The favours, privileges and exemptions of the emperor bound the church to Roman authority, to the point that it was compromised with a totalitarian state, isolated from a people oppressed by taxation. The protection of the empire proved a burden when the emperor intervened in the affairs of the church and convened the first ecumenical council at Nicaea, in the imperial palace.

2. The theological crisis: Arianism

In the third century, Alexandria had established links between faith and theology, despite – or perhaps because of – heterodox Gnosticism. There the priest Arius provoked a new controversy which took his name, imperilling the essence of Christian faith: the divinity of Christ, Son of God.

Some three hundred bishops, for the most part from the East, responded to the imperial call. With the exception of two of them, all signed the Nicene Creed, which we still say in the expanded form authorized by the Council of Constantinople, affirming that Christ is 'very God of very God, of the same substance (*homoousios*) as the Father'.

Agape, Irene and Chionia

The Governor Dulcitius was sitting on the rostrum.
The Governor: Are there not writings, parchments or books among you belonging to these impious Christians?
Chionia: No, sir, the emperors have confiscated them all.
The Governor: Who inspired you to offer this resistance?
Chionia: Almighty God.
The Governor: Who has drawn you into this madness?
Chionia: The Almighty God and his only Son, our Saviour Jesus Christ.
Then he read her the text of the sentence:
'Given that the aforesaid Agape and Chionia have resisted in a spirit of impiety and rebellion against the divine edicts of our sovereigns, the emperors and Caesars, and have continued to practise the Christian religion to this day, that vain and corrupt religion which is hateful to all pious men, we ordain that they be consigned to the flames.' Then he added: 'Agathon, Irene, Cassia, Philippa and Eutychia, by reason of their age, shall be imprisoned until the new order.'
   So died the holy martyrs Agape and Chionia at the stake.

Arianism spread in the East only with the connivance and action of the emperors. Constans proved to be the harbinger of the division and the heresy which were condemned at Nicaea. Theodosius, who was better advised, endorsed the downfall of Arianism by a return to the faith of Nicaea at the Council of Constantinople in 381. Political intervention disrupted the church throughout the fourth century.

3. The inner life of the community

On the other hand, religious peace allowed the church to perfect its organization and multiply first dioceses and then parishes, to develop and establish a structure. It is worth noting that most of the fathers are bishops, responsible for catechesis, liturgy and preaching.

The influx of candidates led to a well organized catechumenate, and biblical, baptismal and mystagogic catechesis. All the fathers of the time contributed towards enriching the literature of Christian initiation.

Improvisation was followed by the age of the great liturgies in the East and even in the West: Basil and Ambrose show the creativity of the time. A Christian poetry was born. The liturgical year saw the organization of Lent, as preparation for baptism and the reconciliation of penitents. The period of three days of preparation for Easter was solemnized: the Paschal night was regarded as 'the fairest of all nights', for the newly baptized and the community who were gathered together.

The cult of martyrs developed in the fourth century. *Martyria* were built over their remains (relics), and became places of pilgrimage throughout the Eastern provinces. In Rome people visited the tombs of Peter and Paul, in Carthage that of Cyprian and in Nola that of Felix. The transfer of relics was the occasion for great festivities.

The same century also saw the blossoming of monastic life, first in the East, in the form of the solitary life, with Antony in Egypt, and then in a communal form, with Pachomius. A more cultivated form appeared in Cappadocia with Basil the Great.

In the West, Rome, Milan, Trier, Hadrumeta, Tours and Rouen experienced a similar rapid development, inspired from the East. Martin of Tours is the prototype of Western monasticism. Augustine produced the first legislation for it. In the next century, Marseilles and Lérins were to intensify the monastic fervour and become theological and missionary centres.

Letter from Constantine to the Governor of Bithynia, traditionally called the Edict of Milan

When I, Constantine Augustus, and I also, Licinius Augustus, had met together in happy circumstances in Milan, to discuss all matters relating to the public good and security, we decided that those things among others which we saw would be to the advantage of many should be ordained first of all, namely the basis for reverence to the deity. We believed that we should give to Christians, as to all men, the freedom to follow the religion of their choice, so that whatever deity there may be in the heavenly regions may be gracious and propitious to us and to all who live under our government. We have therefore determined that with a sound and most upright intent we should take the decision not to deny this possibility to anyone who has attached his soul to the religion of the Christians or that religion which he believes to suit him the best, so that the supreme deity, to whom spontaneously we pay homage, may be able to show us his customary favour and benevolence in all things. Therefore it is fitting that your Excellency should know that we have decided completely to abolish all the restrictions contained in earlier letters sent to your office with reference to Christians and to abolish stipulations which seem to us severe and alien to our mercy. Henceforth we allow all those who have the wish to observe the religion of the Christians to do so freely and completely, without any worry or molestation.

Contained in Lactantius, *The Deaths of the Persecutors*, ch. 48

The Ecumenical Councils of Antiquity

1. Nicaea (325)

Provoked by the affirmations of Arius, according to whom Christ had been 'created'. The Council affirmed that the Word incarnate is of the same substance (*homoousios*, consubstantial) as the Father, God born of God.

2. Constantinople (381)

Strove to put an end to Arianism by reaffirming the divinity of Christ and the divinity of the Holy Spirit, which had been contested by Eunomius. The text has been lost.

3. Ephesus (431)

No definition emerged from the Council. In 433, an 'Act of Union' said: 'Thus we confess Our Saviour Jesus Christ, only Son of God, perfect God and perfect man, composed of a rational soul and body, begotten of the Father before all ages according to his divinity and born in these last days of the Virgin Mary.'

4. Chalcedon (451)

Reacted against Monophysitism (belief that there was only one nature in Christ) and affirmed 'one and the same Son, our Saviour Jesus Christ, perfect in his divinity and perfect in his humanity, truly God and truly man'.

5. Constantinople II (453)

Condemned the errors attributed to Origen and to three theologians (Theodore of Mopsuestia, Theodoret of Cyrrhus and Ibas). Pope Leo I endorsed the condemnation of the errors but not those of the persons. The Council was mainly aimed against Nestorianism.

The First Ecumenical Council, Nicaea 325

The most distinguished of God's ministers from all the churches which abounded in Europe, Libya and Asia were here assembled. And a single house of prayer, as though divinely enlarged, sufficed to contain at once both Syrians and Cilicians, Phoenicians and Arabians, delegates from Palestine and others from Egypt; Thebans and Libyans, with those who came from the region of Mesopotamia. A Persian bishop too was present at this conference, nor was even a Scythian found wanting to the number. Pontus, Galatia and Pamphylia, Cappadocia, Asia and Phrygia, furnished their most distinguished prelates; while those who dwelt in the remotest districts of Thrace and Macedonia, of Achaea and Epirus, were also in attendance. Even from Spain itself, one whose fame was widely spread [Hosius] took his seat as an individual in the great assembly. The bishop of the imperial city [Rome] was prevented from attending by extreme old age; but his presbyters were present, and took his place.

The bishops entered the great hall of the palace and occupied the seats which had been prepared for them, according to their rank . . . When the signal announcing the emperor's entrance was heard, all the bishops rose, and at that hour he entered in the midst of an escort of persons of quality. He appeared like an angel of God, clothed in raiment which glittered as it were with rays of light, reflecting the glowing radiance of a purple robe, and adorned with the brilliant splendour of gold and precious stones.

[Towards the end of the council] he completed the twentieth year of his reign. On this occasion public festivals were celebrated by the people of the provinces generally, but the emperor himself invited and feasted with those ministers of God whom he had reconciled . . . Not one of the bishops was absent from the imperial banquet, the circumstances of which were splendid beyond description. Detachments of the bodyguard and other troops surrounded the entrance of the palace with drawn swords, and through the midst of these the men of God proceeded without fear into the innermost of the imperial apartments, in which some were the emperor's own companions at table, while others reclined on couches arranged on either side. One might have thought that this was a foreshadowing of Christ's kingdom, and the event seemed a dream rather than reality.

After the celebration of this brilliant festival, the emperor courteously received all his guests, and generously added to the favours that he had already bestowed by personally presenting gifts to each individual according to his rank.

Eusebius, *Life of Constantine*, III, 7, 10, 15

The Faith of Nicaea

*The Nicene Creed, compared with the baptismal creed of Caesarea in Palestine,
which served as a basis for it.*

The phrases in italics were introduced against Arius

Creed of Caesarea

We believe in one God,
the Father almighty,
maker of all things
visible and invisible
and in one Lord Jesus Christ,
the Word of God,

God from God,
light from light,
life from life,
the only Son,
first born of all creation,
begotten of the Father before
         all worlds,
by whom all things were made.

For our salvation

he took flesh and dwelt among us.
He suffered,
he rose again on the third day,
he ascended to the Father
and will come again in his glory
to judge the living and the dead.
We also believe in one Holy Spirit.

Nicene Creed

We believe in one God,
the Father almighty,
maker of all things,
visible and invisible,
and in one Lord Jesus Christ,
the Son of God,
begotten from the Father,
only-begotten,
that is from the substance
         of the Father,
God from God,
light from light,
true God from true God,

begotten, *not made,*
consubstantial with the Father,

by whom all things were made
in heaven and on earth.
For us men
and for our salvation
he descended,
was made flesh and made man.
He suffered,
he rose again on the third day,
he ascended into heaven
whence he will come again
to judge the living and the dead.
And in the Holy Spirit.

As for those who say:
there was a time
when he was not, or:
he was not before being begotten,
or: he came forth from nothing,
or that the Son of God
is of another substance or
         essence,
or that he was created
or that he is not immutable
but subject to change,
these the church anathematizes.

II · The Memory of the Church: Eusebius of Caesarea

Eusebius (263–339) forms a hinge between the third and the fourth centuries. He experienced the peace of the church, then the persecution of Diocletian, the return of imperial authority at the moment when he became Bishop of Caesarea in Palestine, the reign of Constantine, the Council of Nicaea and the development of the Arian crisis.

1. A disciple of Origen

Eusebius was trained in Caesarea, where Pamphilus continued Origen's teaching and method. Pamphilus preserved Origen's manuscripts and brought together scattered writings, organizing around the 'Origen foundation' the richest library of Christian writings in antiquity. A community gathered in his house, devoted to study and asceticism. The community specialized in the copying of texts. Later Constantine ordered fifty Bibles on parchment from it for the churches of Constantinople.

In Caesarea, master and disciple produced an *Apologia for Origen*, who was contested in Palestinian circles. Of its six books, only one, the first, has come down to us. After the death of Pamphilus, Eusebius wrote his life; then, however, he was forced to flee to Egypt. On his return to Caesarea he was elected bishop of the city.

2. The man whom Constantine trusted

Eusebius refused to take sides against Arius. A lover of compromise, more a diplomat than a theologian, at Nicaea the Bishop of Caesarea put forward an equivocal formula and subscribed to the decisions of the council only with reluctance. He took part in the cabal against the Nicene party and the council which deposed Athanasius. He became influential with the return of Constantine, on whom he wrote a panegyric. His reputation suffered as a result of these regrettable compromises.

More an apologist than a theologian, Eusebius was above all a historian, and as such performed an indispensable service for the church. His *Church History*, in ten volumes, produced before 325, runs from the foundation of the church to Constantine's victory over Licinius in 324. Eusebius brought together, sometimes in a rather muddled way, a quantity of first-hand documents which are an inexhaustible mine of information on the history of Christian antiquity. His history was later continued by Socrates, then by Sozomen. To it he added as an appendix a work *On the Martyrs of Palestine* which reports eight years of persecution at Caesarea and the martyrdoms of numerous Christians which he witnessed.

Preface to the *Church History*

But this book must crave a lenient judgment from indulgent readers. I confess that it is beyond my powers to fulfil my promise completely and without omission. For I am the first to attempt this work and to venture as it were to travel along a lonely and untrodden path. So I pray that I may have God as my guide and the power of the Lord as my helper; on the human side, however, it is impossible to discover the clear tracks of anyone who has gone before along the same road. I can discover only faint traces of those who, each in his own way, has left behind a partial account of the times through which they passed. Their words are like torches held up ahead, like the cries of watchmen who, from the summit of some tower, indicate the path which one must tread in order to direct the course of the narrative without error and without danger.

So all that I have deemed profitable for the course I have indicated I have gathered from among the things these same people mention here and there, and I shall attempt to embody them in a historical narrative. I shall be happy if I have saved from oblivion the successions, if not of all the apostles of our Lord, at least of the most renowned of them, in those churches that are still pre-eminent and of note today.

Eusebius, *Church History*, I, 2 and 3

III · The Church Expands Eastwards

Our consideration of the expansion of the gospel westwards should not lead us to lose sight of the fact that from the third century it also moved from Antioch into eastern Syria. One of the first known churches with a baptistery is that of Dura Europos on the Euphrates.

At the beginning of the fourth century the church was solidly planted in Sassanid Mesopotamia. Having been cruelly decimated and deported to Seleucia-Ctesiphon, the 'Persian' church continued to develop along two axes, north and south. The church in the south was persecuted by King Shapuhr II (309–79), who sought to dismantle its structure and put virgins and clergy to death. The episcopal see of Seleucia-Ctesiphon remained vacant for almost forty years (348–388). We still have some of the accounts of the Persian martyrs, a jewel of literature.

After Nisibis was taken by the Persians in 363, many Christians went to settle further west in Roman territory, at Edessa. In this semitic Mesopotamia, the language of the country, Syriac, a branch of eastern Aramaic, became official. A start was made by translating the Bible, in a version known as the Peshitto. The national culture presented itself as an offshoot of Jewish–Christian literature, sheltered from Greek thought.

The Syrian liturgy has preserved the heritage of this church to the present day. Its poetry and music were strongly influenced by Judaism. Many Greek works, now lost, like the baptismal homilies of Theodore of Mopsuestia, exist only in Syriac translations. Thus Syriac literature came to enrich the Greek heritage.

Two men stand out: Aphraat, the first Christian writer of the Persian empire, and the deacon Ephraem. Aphraat belonged to a community of ascetics called 'the sons of the covenant', of which he was the superior. His works which have come down to us are not influenced by any philosophy but are inspired only by scripture. He also composed liturgical hymns to be sung in choir. After being translated into Greek, they passed into the church of Antioch, where they introduced responsorial chants.

1. Ephraem, the lyre of the Holy Spirit (306–373)

Born at Nisibis in Mesopotamia (north-west of Mossoul), of a family which was doubtless already Christian, he was ordained deacon by Bishop James. In 363, when the city fell into the hands of the Persians, he settled in Edessa (Orfa), in Roman territory, where he spent the last ten years of his life. He was the founder of a school, a kind of church seminary and Catholic university, which taught writing, reading, singing and commentary on the scriptures.

2. A witness to Syriac theology

Ephraem is the key witness to a different cultural background from that of all the other fathers, set in an extension of the Judaic and Jewish–Christian thought that we have already analysed. He developed a non-Greek exegesis, close to its Old Testament roots, which has affinities with the school of Antioch. He used the method of the Targums and the Midrash. Moses above all proclaims Christ. This is a three-stage typology, in which the figure is first realized in Christ and the church, a realization which is a promise of future achievement.

Ephraem prefers the polysemy of the symbols of scripture and creation to the abstract concepts of philosophy. He never separates biblical symbolism from cosmic symbolism. The trees in scripture are figures of the cross, but every tree, by its rebirth in spring, symbolizes the mystery of the cross and the promise of the resurrection. The incarnation of Christ justifies this interpretation: the universe is created in the image of the only-begotten Son.

Hymn for the Ascension

On this day, the new and spiritual bread ascended into the heavens.
The mysteries were revealed, in your body,
which ascended as an offering. Blessed be your bread, O Lord!

The Lamb has come to us, from the house of David, the priest from the race of Abraham;
for us he has become the Lamb of God, and for us the new priest.
His body is the victim, his blood our drink. Blessed be the new sacrifice!

From heaven he descended like the light,
from Mary he was born as a divine embryo; from the cross he fell like a fruit,
to heaven he mounted as the firstfruits. Blessed be his will!

You are the oblation of heaven and earth, sacrificed, adored,
 each in turn.
You came to be victim, you ascended as a unique offering,
you ascended, Lord, bearing your sacrifice.

Ephraem Syrus, *Hymn 18*

3. Ephraem's writings

Ephraem's work has two orientations, one polemical and the other didactic. He fights against Manichaeism, Marcion's error and above all against Arianism. Orthodoxy is his constant concern. Of his authentic work we have first of all biblical commentaries on the Old Testament, of which only those on Genesis and Exodus have come down to us. His exegesis is above all literal, verse by verse, and is both typological and paraenetic. He wants to get beyond the letter to discover the spirit, which he calls 'the deep meaning'.

Above all, his poetic work has come down to us: metrical homilies (*memre*), which are rhythmic expansions of the mysteries of the faith. Then there are the hymns proper, called *Carmina Nisibena* (*madrash*); these are composed to be sung by a double choir, strophe and refrain.

This is biblical poetry not only in inspiration but also in its structure and procedures: antithetic parallelism, and the use of discordant concord, as in the Psalms and the Odes of Solomon. For Ephraem, Christ is the living expression of this concord in the discord of his divine and human natures; he is the heart of the reading of scripture, of creation and of history.

IV · Christian Egypt

Egypt, which had long been Christian, was violently shaken by the persecution inflicted by the Emperor Maximin. Eusebius speaks of the 'thousands of people' who died martyrs. We know the names of many bishops, including Thmuis, Phileas and above all Peter, Bishop of Alexandria.

1. The birth of Egyptian monasticism

The heroism of the martyrs gave birth to monastic asceticism, which did its utmost to prolong the fervour. After persecution, the Christians had already withdrawn into the desert to lead a precarious existence. They prepared the way for solitary (anchoritic) monasticism in Egypt, in Syria, in Palestine and as far as Mesopotamia. Paul of Thebes became a hermit in 250.

The father of those who took to the wilderness was the Egyptian Antony (c.251–356). We know his story from the *Life of Antony* written by Athanasius, who knew him; translated into several languages, it was to serve as a charter for all monasticism, both Eastern and Western.

Antony was a well-to-do farmer. At the age of twenty he heard the call of the gospel; he sold his land, gave the proceeds to the poor, and settled on a mountain side. A number of anchorites imitated his example. The hermit sometimes sought solitude, and sometimes returned to society, to colonies of anchorites whom he visited and counselled.

In the spirit of Antony, the hermit is no more than a pious lay person who lives out the gospel in a radical way. A struggle against the spirit of evil into whose power the world has fallen, fasting, vigils, meditation on scripture, absolute poverty, are the means which allow him to attain gospel perfection.

Antony's spiritual teaching is mainly collected in the *Apophthegms* (Sentences) and the *Lausiac History*. Here is an example: 'A solitary, seeing another carrying a dead body, said to him: "My brother, you do well, but you would do even better to support the living."'

By contrast, Pachomius developed pure anchoritism (absolute solitude) or tempered anchoritism (hermits grouped around a spiritual father) in the direction of a cenobitic (communal) life, under the authority of an abbot.

Pachomius began by becoming the disciple of an anchorite, Palaemon; after seven years he felt called to put himself at the service of others. After several barren attempts 'with monks who only wanted to do it in their head', he found his first recruits and developed a communal rule of life (part of which we still have), the essence of which was obedience. He set up his first monastery in Tabennisi (in the region of Thebes). Mary, his sister, asked and obtained his permission to establish a monastery of nuns nearby.

Pachomian monasticism came to be organized in Upper Egypt. Later, Shenoute established the famous community of Athribis, near Thebes. This gave the term Thebaid (district around Thebes) monastic connotations. The two forms continued to co-exist and develop. Anchoritism became established not far from Alexandria and spread up the Nile as far as the desert of Nitria.

2. The church of Alexandria and its bishops

Alexandria was a large church, bustling and effervescent. Its bishop Peter, an old ascetic, died a martyr in 312. Alexander succeeded him in the same year. He was opposed by Arius, an eloquent scholar and an ascetic priest of Baucalis, one of the churches in the city. This opposition centred on trinitarian doctrine, in which Arius stressed subordinationism: the Son is distinctly inferior; he is no more than a divine, perfect creature.

The bishop, who kept a firm hand on the church of Egypt, convened a council of around a hundred bishops and anathematized the statements of Arius. Arius looked for support from Eusebius of Caesarea and Eusebius of Nicomedia (the seat of the emperor), who was an influential figure. Gradually the Christian East found itself split in two. As we have seen, Constantine, the absolute master, decided to convene an ecumenical council at Nicaea. Athanasius, still a deacon, went to it with his bishop, whom he succeeded in 328.

Athanasius, pillar of orthodoxy (296–373)

Athanasius is one of the greatest episcopal figures of antiquity. Hewn in granite, intransigent to the point of violence, he was a bishop of the resistance. He was born in Alexandria, knew the people well, sympathized with their piety, and learned Coptic. He knew how to sway crowds, if need be like a tribune.

A Christian from his infancy, he had a classical education with only elements of philosophy. Some of his teachers died as martyrs under Diocletian, so they were Christians. Athanasius put himself at the service of the church, defending it in an intrepid way, as a son defends his mother.

Life of Antony

First steps in asceticism (270)

On another occasion, as he was going into church, he heard the Lord saying in the Gospel, 'Do not be anxious about the morrow.' He could not bear it any longer, but went out and gave even the little he had left to the needy. Later, entrusting his sister to virgins who were well known and faithful, he put her in a convent to be brought up and then devoted himself to asceticism not far from his own house, watching over himself strictly, and patiently training himself. Monasteries were not yet so common in Egypt, and no monk knew anything of the great desert. Anyone who wanted to see to his soul practised the ascetical life alone, not far from his own village. Thus there was in the neighbouring village at that time an old man who had lived a solitary life from his youth up. Upon seeing him, Antony sought to equal him in virtue, so he too began to stay in the neighbourhood of the village. If he heard talk of a zealous person anywhere else, he would go forth from there like a wise bee and seek him out, and did not return to his own place until he had seen him. After taking from him supplies, as it were, for travelling along the road to virtue, he returned. So it was here that he went through the first stages of asceticism, strengthening his resolve not to return to his inheritance and not to think of his kinsfolk. He directed his whole desire and all his energies to strengthening his spiritual practices. He worked with his hands, for he had heard, 'If any man will not work, neither let him eat', spending part of his wages on bread and distributing the rest to the needy. He prayed continually, because he had learned that one must pray in secret without ceasing. He was so attentive to what he heard read that nothing escaped him, but he remembered everything, his memory later serving him instead of books.

He learns from other ascetics and tries to imitate their virtues

Training himself in this way, Antony was loved by all. He submitted himself willingly to the zealous men whom he went to see and learned from them the zeal and self-denial which each had acquired: he noticed the courtesy of one, the constancy of another in prayer; he observed one's meekness, another's kindness; he attentively watched one as he kept vigil and another in his love of study; he admired one for his patience and another for his fasting and sleeping on the bare ground. In all he noted their devotion to Christ and their love one for another. Having thus gathered his fill, he returned to his own place of solitude, afterwards reflecting on the special virtues of each one and striving eagerly to exemplify all of them in himself. He was envious of his contemporaries on only one point: that he should not be inferior to them in anything. He did this in such a way as to offend no one; rather, everyone felt the joy which he had. And all the villagers and the lovers of the good who knew him, seeing him thus, called him a friend of God. Some loved him as a son, others as a brother.

Athanasius, *Life of Antony*, 3, 4

Defender of the faith of Nicaea   Athanasius was thirty-three years old when, after a laborious election, contested and finally endorsed by the emperor, he became patriarch of the prestigious city of Alexandria in 328. The bishop sought to affirm the faith of Nicaea in his diocese.

In 330 Athanasius clashed both with disciples of the priest Meletius, who professed a rigorist position after the persecutions, and with the supporters of Arius. He categorically refused to reinstate Arius among the clergy of the city despite the emperor's injunction. The Arianizers forced a synod in Tyre in 335 which deposed the patriarch, whereupon the emperor sent him into exile in Trier. This was the first of five banishments.

The Word made Flesh

The Word of God, seeing the human race perishing and death reigning over them by corruption, and seeing also the threat of sin strengthening corruption over us, and deeming that it was out of place for the law to be abolished before it had been fulfilled; seeing also that he could not allow this universe, of which he was himself the Artificer, to vanish away; seeing also the excessive depravity of man, and how it was increasing to such an extent as to become unbearable; seeing, finally, that all men were condemned to death, took pity on our infirm race. Moved by our corruption, and not bearing the tyranny of death, in order that what was made might not perish, and that the work of his Father in forming man might not be in vain, he took a body for himself, a body like ours.

He did not wish simply to be in the body, nor did he wish simply to be seen. For had he wished simply to be visible in a body, he could surely have made a divine manifestation in a more excellent body. But he took our body – not just any body, but from a virgin inviolate and incorrupt, who had not known a man: a body pure and without stain from any human intercourse.

He, the Almighty, the Artificer of the universe, made a temple for himself in the womb of a virgin: his own body. This body he made his own, as the instrument through which he was known and in which he dwelt.

Thus, taking a body like our own, because all were subjected to the corruption of death, in his extreme humility he offered his own body to the Father as a victim of death. Likewise, since all our bodies were liable to the corruption of death, the law of corruption launched against mankind exhausted the power of its sting on the body of the Lord, but then found itself with no power against mankind like to him. Those who had turned back to corruption he made incorruptible: by his incarnation and by the grace of his resurrection, he restored them from death to life, swallowing up death as straw is swallowed up by fire.

Perceiving that corruption could not be abolished otherwise than through death, but also knowing that he himself, the Word, the Son of the Father, could not die, he assumed a mortal body. In this way, united to the Word who is above all, this body was to die also for us, and furthermore, made incorruptible by the Word dwelling within it, would have the power by his resurrection to banish corruption for all others as well. So the Word of God offered his pure body as a victim to death, and at the same time banished that of all bodies like his own. The one who is superior to all offered as a ransom for all his temple and the instrument of his body; by doing this, in his own death he paid our debt.

Since he is united to all men by a body which is like theirs, the incorruptible Son of God can also clothe all men in his own incorruptibility and give them a pledge of their coming resurrection, so that death no longer has any dominion over them, precisely because of the Word who dwells among them in a body like to theirs.

When a powerful king makes an entry into a great city and has chosen a particular house in which to dwell there, this whole city deems itself to be greatly honoured: enemies and robbers cease to attack it and molest it; all judge it worthy of the highest honours because of the king who lives in one of its mansions. So it is with the King of the universe: when he came to our earth and inhabited a body like to ours, all machinations of the enemy of man ceased and even the ancient corruption of death disappeared. The whole human race would have perished completely had not the Son of God, King of the Universe, himself come to snatch it from death and save it.

Athanasius, *Incarnation of the Word*, 8, 9

– First exile, under Constantine, from 11 July 335 to 22 November 337, spent in Trier;
– Second exile, under Constantius, from 16 July 339 to 21 October 346, spent in Rome;
– Third exile, under Constantius, from 9 February 356 to 21 February 362, spent in the desert of Egypt;
– Fourth exile, under Julian, from 24 October 362 to 5 September 363, also spent in the desert of Egypt;
– Fifth exile, under Valens, from 5 October 365 to 31 January 366, also spent in the desert of Egypt.

Athanasius died on 2 May 373. Of the forty-six years of his episcopate he had spent twenty in exile. The most important part of his writings was devoted to a defence of the creed of Nicaea: equality of nature, of substance, of dignity, of the Son and the Father. He first presented this in *Three Discourses against the Arians*. He related the events which had condemned and then rehabilitated Arius in the *Apology against the Arians* and the *History of the Arians*. There he refuted the affirmations of the heresiarch and expounded the faith of Nicaea, which he also professed in letters to the Egyptian bishop Serapion.

The apologist and the polemicist Athanasius was a fighter. In his youth, while still a deacon, he wrote a *Discourse against the Pagans and on the Incarnation of the Word* on the lines of the apologies. In it he refuted idolatry; he showed the foolishness of pagan deities and the way which allows one to reach the true God. To find it there is no other way than man himself, who bears the trace of the God who created him.

In his polemical works provoked by Arianism, like *Apologia for My Flight* and *History of the Arians*, the exiled bishop employs a scathing irony which spares no one. He directs terrible words against the eunuchs who surround the emperor and advise him: 'How can these people understand anything of the generation of the Son of God?' The bishop has the virility of the violent men who take the kingdom of God by force.

The friend of monks Monasteries of anchorites and cenobites flourished from Alexandria to the Thebaid. Athanasius visited them, first out of sympathy and then to take refuge there. He knew Antony and spent time with him before writing his life. Antony intervened with the emperor on behalf

---

The Faith of St Athanasius

So there is one holy and perfect Trinity, acknowledged as God in the Father and the Son and the Holy Spirit; it comprehends nothing alien, nothing that is intermingled with it from outside; it is not made up of creator and created, but is entirely creative and productive virtue; it is like to itself, indivisible by nature, and its workings are one. The Father does all things through the Word in the Spirit, and in this way the unity of the Holy Trinity is safeguarded, just as, in the church, there is proclamation of one God alone, 'who is above all things and through all things and in all things': 'above all things' as Father, as principle and source; 'through all things' by the Word, and 'in all things' in the Holy Spirit. The Trinity exists, not limited to a name and the appearance of a word, but as Trinity and reality. For just as the Father is the One who Is, so too his Word is the One who Is and God above all,

and the Holy Spirit is not deprived of existence, but is and truly exists. The Catholic Church thinks no less, so as to avoid falling among those who are now Jews in the manner of Caiaphas and Sabellius; it imagines no more, to avoid sinking into the polytheism of the Gentiles.

Let this be the faith of the church, and let its enemies learn this by the way in which the Lord, when he sent out the apostles, enjoined them to give this foundation to the church, saying: 'Go teach all nations, baptizing them in the name of the Father, and of the Son, and of the Holy Spirit.' For their part the apostles, when they had gone forth, taught thus, and this is the preaching to be found throughout the church under heaven.

Athanasius, *Letter to Serapion* I, 28

of the bishop. He even went to Alexandria at the request of the Egyptian bishops to refute the errors of Arius in the most formal way.

Athanasius took into exile with him monks who introduced monasticism to the West. Like all the bishops of Alexandria, he knew the influence of monks upon ordinary people. The religious supported not only the authority of the bishop but the orthodox doctrine of Nicaea. Conversely, the patriarch of Alexandria was both a witness and propagandist and the spiritual author of monastic asceticism. He wrote a treatise *On Virginity* and kept up a correspondence with the virgins of Alexandria. The *Life of Antony* was not only a best-seller but the charter for all monasticism.

Cyril of Alexandria (died 444)

If Athanasius illustrates the first part of the fourth century, Theophilus, one of his successors, was a most colourful figure, a real Christian pharaoh, concerned above all to pit his power against that of his rival, Constantinople. He fought against pagan cults, destroying the temples of Serapis (with its library), Mithras and Dionysus. At first an admirer of Origen, opportunistically he ended up by changing camps in order to reconcile himself with the anti-Origenist monks.

Theophilus played a sadly famous role in the condemnation of John Chrysostom to exile. This provoked the break with Rome. He was not content to rule over all Egypt for his lifetime, but prepared for his successor. His own nephew Cyril was elected, not without difficulty, on 15 October 412.

The new bishop had a formidable advantage over his uncle: he knew theology. In the first part of his episcopate he wrote polemic against the Arians in the wake of Athanasius. More than a third of his voluminous book *Treasury of the Holy and Consubstantial Trinity* consisted of extracts from Athanasius on this subject.

Cyril's familiarity with scripture did not in any way prevent him from preferring the strong manner of his uncle to the gentleness of the gospel. He instigated a pogrom which did away with the great Jewish colony in the city. He was also accused of connivance in the murder of a pagan woman, the highly esteemed philosopher Hypatia. He divided his time between pastoral care and his theological work until 428.

Cyril and the Council of Ephesus Arianism led the church to put the emphasis on the divinity of Christ. However, this introduced the risk of minimizing his human nature. Apollinarius, bishop of Laodicea, went too far in this direction, asserting that Christ did not have a human soul, and only one nature, a divine nature.

The vocabulary of the period was far from having the precision it has today with which to maintain the unity of person in Christ in the duality of the two natures, divine and human. The notions of complete nature and hypostasis, which the Latins called *persona* (person), did not have their present clarity, and this led to confusion.

The truth – but not human beings – kept the two extremes equidistant. Two schools or currents which should have been complementary, clashed: the confrontation was aggravated by rivalries between sees and by the passion of the metropolitans.

Nestorius, a monk of Antioch who became Bishop of Constantinople, lit the touch-paper by criticizing the title 'Theotokos', Mother of God, which had been given to Mary. The expression was clearly orthodox only if one understood it to refer to the person of Jesus and not his nature: Mary is the mother of a man who is the Son of God. It is impossible to speak of two sons.

In reality, Cyril's talk of a 'physical unity' or of the 'unique nature of the Logos made flesh' was unfortunate. This formula of Apollinarius which circulated under the name of Athanasius was a falsification by which Cyril was unhappily deceived, amalgamating nature and hypostasis.

Instead of clarification, the consequence was a cabal. Cyril took a stand in a paschal letter, calling on Nestorius to retract. He referred the matter to Pope Innocent I. A Roman synod required Nestorius to recant, on pain of deposition. Cyril transmitted the Roman sentence, but added to it twelve anathemas of his own devising, which were theologically questionable.

The Emperor Theodosius II, who was hostile to

Cyril of Alexandria:
Homily Given at the Council of Ephesus (431)

I see this joyful assembly of holy bishops who, at the invitation of the blessed Mother of God, Mary ever Virgin, have gathered here with enthusiasm. And although I am sad, the presence of these holy Fathers fills me with joy. Among us are fulfilled the sweet words of the psalmist David: 'Behold how good and sweet it is, brethren, to dwell together in unity.'

So we hail you, mysterious holy Trinity, who have brought us all together in this church of holy Mary Mother of God.

We hail you, Mary, Mother of God, sacred treasure of all the universe, star who never sets, crown of virginity, sceptre of the orthodox law, indestructible temple, dwelling-place of the incommensurable Mother and Virgin, for the sake of the one who is called 'blessed' in the holy Gospels, the one who 'comes in the name of the Lord'.

We hail you, who held in your virginal womb him whom the heavens cannot contain; through whom the Trinity is glorified and worshipped throughout the earth; through whom the heavens exult; through whom the angels and archangels rejoice; through whom the demons are put to flight; through whom the tempter fell from heaven; through whom the fallen creation is raised to the heavens; through whom the whole world, held captive by idolatry, has come to know the truth; through whom holy baptism is given to those who believe, with 'the oil of gladness'; through whom churches have been founded throughout the world; through whom pagan nations have been led to conversion.

What more shall I say? It is through you that the light of the only-begotten Son of God has shone 'for those who dwelt in darkness and in the shadow of death'; it is through you that the prophets proclaimed the future, that the apostles preach salvation to the nations, that the dead are raised and that kings reign, in the name of the holy Trinity.

Is there a single person who can worthily celebrate the praises of Mary? She is both mother and virgin. What a marvel! A marvel which overwhelms me! Who has ever heard it said that the builder was prevented from dwelling in the temple which he himself built? Should one criticize him who gave his servant the title of mother?

Thus the whole world rejoices. May it be given us to worship and adore the unity, to worship and honour the indivisible Trinity, by singing the praises of Mary ever virgin, that is the holy church, and those of her Son and immaculate Spouse, to whom be glory for ever and ever, Amen.

Formula of Union, 433

Thus we confess our Lord Jesus Christ, only-begotten Son of God, perfect God and perfect man, composed of a rational soul and a body, begotten of the Father before all ages according to his divinity, born in these last days, for us and for our salvation, of the Virgin Mary according to his humanity; consubstantial with the Father according to his divinity, consubstantial with us according to his humanity. For the union is made of two natures. That is why we affirm one Christ, one Son, one Lord. By reason of this union without confusion, we confess the holy Virgin Mother of God, because God the Word was incarnate and made man, and from the moment of his conception was united with the temple which he had taken from her. As for the words of the Gospels and the apostles about the Lord, we know that theologians have sometimes grouped them as sayings about a single person and sometimes separated them as being said about two natures: some befitting God, according to the divinity of Christ; the others humble, according to his humanity.

Cyril, convened an ecumenical council at Ephesus. At the first session, for which the Syrian bishops had not yet arrived, Cyril made haste to have Nestorius condemned. When they did arrive, John of Antioch and the Syrian bishops excommunicated Cyril. The Roman legates disembarked in their turn and approved the decision of the first session. The emperor confirmed the deposition of the two antagonists, Nestorius and Cyril.

Cyril's skill allowed him to regain his liberty and his see, while Nestorius was banished to a monastery in Antioch. Cyril felt that the time for concessions had come and renounced his anathemas. Union was finally achieved in 433 on the basis of a formula which Pope Sixtus III approved.

Cyril's doctrinal work All his life the Bishop of Alexandria remained a studious man, anxious to discern the teaching of scripture and tradition. The theological work of this patriarch, harassed by a multitude of tasks, remains one of the most extensive in the Christian East. Cyril was a man of dogmatic affirmation: in both theology and government he proceeded in an authoritarian way.

He has left us a monumental and sometimes prolix commentary on the Gospel of John in twelve volumes, more polemical and doctrinal than exegetical, which contains a number of theological excursuses. His vigour comes from his biblical roots. In an applied reading of scripture, Cyril drew on a faith which was utterly certain of itself.

His investigation covers the books of the Old and New Testaments, above all in two works, *Adoration in Spirit and Truth* and the *Glaphyrae* (Engravings). Cyril seeks harmony between the two Testaments, seeing the Old Testament as the preparation for the Gospel, beginning with Adam and marking the way to the Messiah. Persons and events prophesy the coming of the Word made flesh. To these two works one can add the 156 *Homilies on Luke*.

The incarnation lies at the heart of Cyril's theology and economy. He rejects Nestorian dualism with all his might, so as to affirm the unity of Christ. But his christology leaves the human nature of Jesus and the autonomy of his activities blurred. Mixing up the concepts of nature and hypostasis, Cyril's theological vocabulary lacks rigour, to the point that he can even speak of the 'sole nature of Christ'. The Greek philosophy which he criticized in Origen would have allowed him to formulate his views more rigorously.

V · Jerusalem, the City of Witness

The Romans had built a new city, Aelia Capitolina, in which the Temple gave way to the Capitol. A Christian community of Gentile origin formed again there. We know of a bishop from the end of the second century. Eusebius of Caesarea reports that the faithful were sorely tested by the persecutions of Diocletian and Maximin, in two successive waves.

The Council of Nicaea gave the titular bishop a primacy of honour, because Jerusalem was the mother of all the churches. This led to friction with the metropolitan of Caesarea. Constantine had the Holy Sepulchre enclosed in a rotunda, the Anastasis or Church of the Resurrection. It was there that Cyril gave his famous catecheses when he was still only a priest. The empress Helena in turn had two basilicas built, one on the Mount of Olives and the other in Bethlehem: the latter still exists.

1. Cyril of Jerusalem (313–387)

Cyril was almost certainly born in Jerusalem. To judge from his skill as an orator, he must have received a good education there. Around 343 he was ordained priest by Bishop Maximus, a confessor of the faith, who had returned from the mines lame and blind in one eye. On Maximus' death in 350 Cyril was duly elected bishop and installed with the consent of the metropolitan.

The next year, a dispute brought him into conflict with his metropolitan Acacius, who charged him with having sold sacred objects in a time of famine. This was no more than a pretext, the real reason being that Acacius had made a pact with the Arians. The metropolitan then convened a synod which deposed Cyril. Cyril resisted. Acacius came with a gang to expel him by force of arms and install an Arian prelate. During thirty-eight years as a bishop,

Cyril spent sixteen years in three exiles, far from Jerusalem.

– First exile under Constans   357–359
– Second exile under Constantius   359–362
– Third exile under Valens   367–378

Cyril spent the last years of his life bandaging wounds and re-establishing unity in a city divided into Arians and orthodox, in order to give a dignity to the city of Jesus in the sight of the pilgrims who flooded to it. We know from Gregory of Nyssa how much its reputation had been compromised.

The Bishop of Jerusalem, like the Bishops of Alexandria and Poitiers, had suffered persecution for his orthodoxy and a faith based on the Council of Nicaea. Less of a fighter than Athanasius, less of a theologian than Hilary, Cyril had the quiet strength of faith, constancy under trial, and a concern for charity and unity in the truth. 'Error', he was accustomed to say, 'has many forms, but truth has only one face.'

Cyril the catechist

The fourth century is the golden age of baptismal catechesis. Cyril is the equal of Ambrose, Augustine and John Chrysostom. We have the good fortune still to have his complete explanation of the creed, in nineteen catecheses, followed by five others, which are called 'mystagogical', because they are an explanation of the three sacraments of Christian initiation, all administered on Easter Eve.

The baptismal catecheses

During the course of Lent the bishop – or rather, the priest – first unfolded the great stages of biblical history which proclaim Christ and the church. The prophecies of the old covenant are matched by the sacraments in the new covenant. The catechist then explained in a basic but complete way the truths of faith, summarized in the baptismal confession of the creed. After an introduction, Cyril explains the ten dogmas of the faith article by article: God the Father, the only-begotten Son, the incarnation, the cross, the resurrection and the ascension, the end of the ages, the Holy Spirit, the resurrection of the flesh, the church, eternal life.

Cyril preached his homilies to the catechumens near to the tomb of Jesus, in the great Constantinian

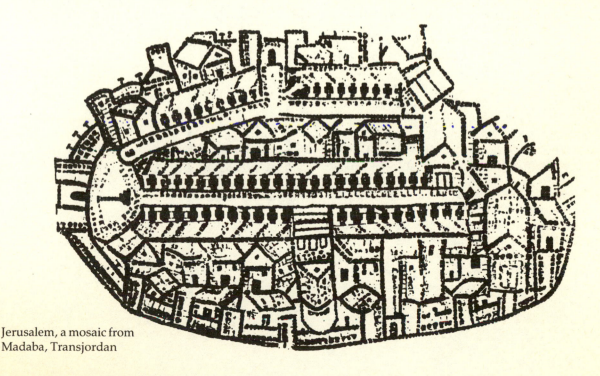

Jerusalem, a mosaic from Madaba, Transjordan

basilica not far from Calvary: 'On the very site of Golgotha we are giving our exposition of Christ and Golgotha' (16.4). He adds: 'Every action of Christ is the glory of the catholic church, but the glory of glories is the cross.'

The mystagogical catecheses

Whether they come from Cyril or from his successor John does not affect the content of the five catecheses in any way. Given after baptism during Easter week, they are much shorter than the previous ones. 'In these catecheses you will be taught the reasons and justifications for each of the rites, according to the Old and New Testaments.' Here we find sacramental typology – the crossing of the Red Sea as a proclamation of baptism, the manna as a figure of the eucharist – and an explanation of the main liturgical rites.

These homilies are 'one of the most precious documents from Christian antiquity'. Thanks to Cyril, we have a glimpse of the liturgy in Jerusalem and a specimen of baptismal catechesis and mystagogical theory.

2. Jerusalem, a pilgrimage centre

With the Constantinian era Jerusalem and the holy places of Palestine, adorned with sumptuous buildings, exercised a great attraction. Monks settled there, first in solitary cells and then in real convents. At Jerusalem, to maintain the office, the monks formed the original nucleus and were joined by nuns, clergy and laity.

There were not only Eastern but also Western monasteries there, after Rufinus of Aquileia with Melania the Elder founded a convent which welcomed 'bishops, monks and virgins'. The same thing happened in Bethlehem, where Jerome established a twofold ascetic community of men and women, with Paula of Rome and her daughter Eustochium.

The historians of the time, like Eusebius and Jerome, give us information about the holy places and the course of pilgrimages. We have a variety of itineraries, including one from Bordeaux to Jerusalem, and more particularly descriptions of the holy

The Church of the Nativity, a view from the entrance on the lower left-hand side

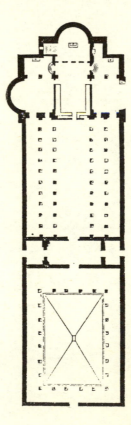

Plan of the Church of the Nativity in Bethlehem

74

Mystagogical Catechesis

For the newly baptized. There is a reading from the First Catholic Epistle of Saint Peter, beginning from 'Be sober, be watchful' to the end.

It has long been my wish, true born and long-desired children of the church, to discourse to you about these spiritual and heavenly mysteries. But knowing that seeing is believing, I waited until the present occasion, reckoning that after what you have experienced you would be a readier audience, now that I am to guide you to the brighter and more fragrant meadows of this paradise.

In particular, you are now capable of understanding the more divine mysteries of divine and life-giving baptism. So now that the time has come to prepare for you the table of more perfect instruction, let me explain the significance of what happened to you on the evening of your baptism.

First you entered the antechamber of the baptistery and faced towards the west. When you were commanded to stretch out your hands, you renounced Satan as though he were there in person.

Now you should know that this moment is prefigured in ancient history. When Pharaoh, the harshest and most cruel of all tyrants, was oppressing the free and noble people of the Hebrews, God sent Moses to deliver them from the hard slavery imposed on them by the Egyptians. They anointed their doorposts with the blood of a lamb, that the destroyer might pass over the houses signed with the blood; so the Hebrew people was miraculously liberated.

After their liberation the enemy gave chase, and on seeing the sea part miraculously before them, they still continued in hot pursuit, only to be immediately engulfed in the Red Sea.

Let us now pass from the old to the new, from the figure to the reality. There Moses is sent by God to Egypt; here Christ is sent by the Father into the world. Moses' mission was to lead an oppressed people from Egypt; here the Christ will deliver those who are under the tyranny of sin.

There the blood of the lamb turned away the exterminator; here the blood of the unspotted lamb, Jesus Christ, puts the demons to flight. The tyrant pursued the ancient Hebrew people right to the sea; this outrageous spirit, the impudent author of all evil, followed each one of you up to the edge of the saving streams. That other tyrant was engulfed in the sea; this one disappears in the saving waters.

Cyril of Jerusalem, *First Mystagogical Lecture*, 1–3

city. Some works are anonymous and some are not; notable among the latter is the diary of Egeria.

The pilgrims came from all over the world. First of all they came from the neighbourhood: the faithful flooded into Jerusalem from surrounding places at festivals. From the fourth century onwards a cosmopolitan population visited the holy places. The numbers from the West were impressive. People came from Africa, from Spain, from Gaul, from Italy and from Pannonia, often setting out on the prompting of Jerome, who ended up by complaining at their numbers.

The monks were the most numerous: 'We are submerged by hordes of monks who come from every part of the world,' writes Jerome. Then came bishops and laity of high rank. If abuses could creep in, as Gregory of Nyssa reports, the majority of pilgrims arrived in a movement of faith, to pray, to edify and instruct themselves, and to do penance. Some stayed there, others wanted to be buried in the holy places. In Jerusalem the pilgrims were buried by the valley of Jehoshaphat.

Egeria's travel diary

We have an exceptional source of information about Jerusalem, and pilgrimages to the holy places of the East, in the diary of someone who is difficult to put in context, Egeria. She was an educated woman attached to a community which seems to have been more a beguinage than a monastery. Her first editor thought that she came from Gaul and her latest leans more towards Galicia.

The diary, which covers the years from 381 to 384, is of the utmost interest because it gives us information about the topography of important places (the Holy Sepulchre, Zion, the Mount of Olives, Bethlehem, Bethany). It informs us about the liturgical year, principally about the celebration of Easter; about daily celebrations, fasts and catechesis. The book is full of information about ecclesiastical organization (bishop, priests, deacons, deaconesses), and about a variety of monastic settlements of men and women outside Palestine: on Sinai, and in Egypt, Syria and Mesopotamia. Finally, the author writes a Latin 'with a common colouring', close to the earliest Latin translation of the Bible.

VI · The Influence of Christian Cappadocia

Cappadocia lies at the heart of present-day Turkey, where the rock churches still bear witness even now to the vitality of Christianity in antiquity. After the Emperor Tiberius annexed this distant province, Rome built a capital on the model of the great cities, with baths, a theatre and festivals, and gave it the name of Caesar, Caesarea (Kayseri).

The region was evangelized very early on, since the letter of Peter is already addressed to its Christians. Tertullian mentions a persecution which went on in his time. Cyprian corresponded with Firmilian, Bishop of Caesarea. A Cappadocian contemporary became Bishop of Jerusalem. A disciple of Origen, Gregory Thaumaturgus, who came from Neocaesarea on the Black Sea, devoted himself to evangelization and became bishop of his native city. Seven Cappadocian bishops were present at the Council of Nicaea in 325.

The great persecution of Galerius and Maximin Daia had struck the province of Pontus harshly. It lasted from 303 to 313. The family of Basil (of Caesarea) and his younger brother Gregory (of Nyssa) give us an example of the ill-treatment suffered by influential and well-to-do Christians. Their grandparents on their father's side, reputable and rich, had had to flee into the forests of Pontus.

Their grandmother's family had heaped up civil and military offices, and were also dignitaries at the imperial court. Their maternal grandfather died a martyr, and all his goods were confiscated after his death. The two brothers, along with Gregory of Nazianzus, were to shed incomparable glory on the church. History unites them under the name of the three Cappadocians.

1. Basil of Caesarea (329–379)

Ten children were born to Emmelia and Basil, a brilliant and rich orator of Neocaesarea who watched over the intellectual and spiritual upbringing of the family until his premature death around 341. Macrina was the oldest, and Peter, the future Bishop of Sebaste, the youngest. Basil, the second child and first son, was born around 329.

Fragile by nature, the oldest of the boys had attention lavished on him. Amazingly gifted, and educated first by his father, he went to Caesarea to finish his studies. There he made friends with Gregory of Nazianzus, and then travelled to make the acquaintance of the masters of Constantinople and Athens.

On his return, Basil established himself as an

Arles, Museum of
Christian Sculpture

orator in Caesarea and taught with great verve.
Carried away by his success, he had to be reminded
of the essentials by his sister Macrina. 'He awoke as
from a deep sleep', gave up his position, received
baptism at the hands of the bishop, and then
plunged into solitude, putting himself to school
with the monks first of Egypt and Palestine, then of
Mesopotamia.

The ascetic life permanently damaged his health.
Then he returned home to distribute his fortune to
the poor and settle in the solitude of Annesi, on the
banks of the Iris, where Gregory of Nazianzus came
to join him. Together they composed an anthology
of texts by Origen called the *Philocalia* ('I love
flowers'). And there in solitude Basil framed two
monastic rules.

Ordained priest in Caesarea, Basil ended up by
settling and working there until the death of Bishop
Eusebius, whom he succeeded in 370 after a somewhat laborious election because of his health. 'Do
you have to be an athlete or a doctor of the faith?'
someone remarked. Nine years were enough for
this forty-year-old to earn the title 'Great' in his
lifetime. From now on his biography and his actions
merge.

The defender of the faith of Nicaea

Basil had been strangely prepared to become a
theologian of high calibre. His pastoral work and
his brief career left him little time to develop his
theological writings. At least he demonstrated the
propaedeutic place of classical culture in a long
letter to his nephews, which has remained famous
because of its moderate and open attitude to the
Greek heritage: 'You must imitate the bees: gather
the honey and leave the poison.' This was a text
which was to delight the Renaissance.

The Arian crisis into which the whole church had

The Nature of the Spirit

First of all, who, on hearing the titles of the Spirit, is not lifted up in soul? Who does not elevate his thought to the supreme nature? He is called Spirit of God, 'Spirit of truth which proceeds from the Father' (John 15.26), 'right Spirit' (Ps. 50.12), 'sovereign Spirit' (Ps. 50.14). His proper and peculiar title is 'Holy Spirit', which is a name specially appropriate to all that is incorporeal, purely immaterial and indivisible. That is why the Lord, when teaching the woman who thought God to be an object of local worship that the incorporeal cannot be circumscribed, said, 'God the Spirit' (John 4.24). So it is not possible when one hears this name of Spirit to imagine a nature circumscribed, subject to change and variation, or at all like the creature. On the contrary, we have to raise our thought to the highest level and think of a substance endowed with intelligence, of infinite power, of a greatness which knows no limit, which cannot be measured in times or ages, and which lavishes its good gifts.

To the Spirit turn all those who are in need of sanctification; all those seek him who live by virtue, for his breath refreshes them and comes to their aid in the pursuit of their natural and proper end. Capable of perfecting others, the Spirit himself lacks nothing. He is not a being who needs to restore its strength, but himself supplies life; he does not grow by additions, but possesses abundant fullness; he abides in himself, but is also present everywhere. The source of sanctification, a light perceptible to the mind, he supplies through himself illumination to every force of reason in quest of the truth. By nature inaccessible, he can be understood by reason of his goodness; filling all things with his power, he communicates himself only to those who are worthy of him, not by sharing himself according to a unique measure but by distributing his energy in proportion to faith. Simple in essence, varied in his miracles, he is wholly present to everyone and wholly everywhere at the same time. He is shared without being affected; he remains whole and yet gives himself in the sharing, like a sunbeam whose kindly light shines on the one who enjoys it as though it shone for him alone, yet lights land and sea and mingles with the air.

Similarly, the Spirit is present to all those who are capable of receiving him as though given to them alone, and yet he sends forth full and sufficient grace for all mankind, and is enjoyed by all who share in him, according to the capacity, not of his power but of their nature.

Souls in which the Spirit dwells, illuminated by the Spirit, themselves become spiritual and send forth their grace to others. From here comes foreknowledge of the future, understanding of mysteries, apprehension of what is hidden, the sharing of the gifts of grace, heavenly citizenship, a place in the chorus of angels, joy without end, abiding in God, being made like God and, highest of all, being made God.

Basil of Caesarea, *Treatise on the Holy Spirit*, 9

been plunged by the emperor's action first led Basil forcefully to resist the pressure of the Emperor Valens. It provided him with the occasion for writing two dogmatic works. One was against Eunomius, a Cappadocian, Bishop of Cyzicus on the Black Sea, who professed a radical Arianism called anomoianism: the Father alone is God, and his Son is only a creature. In his refutation, Basil reaffirmed the perfect equality of the Son and the Spirit with the Father. The *Treatise on the Holy Spirit*, a masterpiece, is not limited to affirming the divinity of the Spirit, but gives an admirable description of his action in faith, liturgy, prayer and the everyday life of the church.

The social bishop

The Bishop of Caesarea was a pioneer and a precursor of social action, in both his writings and his achievements. Witnessing an impoverished empire whose taxation was driving colonists and ordinary people to the wall, and where the cancer of usury was rife, the bishop developed the great social themes: the fundamental equality of all human beings before God, the eminent worth of every human being, the need for a redistribution of goods to limit greed and the enrichment of only some, to put an end to social injustice and the wretchedness of others.

Basil was not content to preach against luxury, avarice and usury in season and out of season, but also devoted himself to social and charitable work. So he built a veritable city, the Basiliad, with a hostelry, a hospice for old people and a hospital which had an area reserved for those with contagious diseases, and finally lodgings for employees and workers. This proved to be a real workers' city, an economic furnace. Basil was one of the first social apostles raised up by the church.

The father of monasticism

Like most of the great converts, Basil 'entered into religion', i.e. he became a monk when he was converted. Living amongst religious, he knew monasticism from within: its greatness and its weaknesses. His action was a commendation of communal life, in order to avoid the eccentricities of

A *librarius* replacing a scroll in the *armarium*

certain anchorites and promote an effort that was both theological and exegetical.

What are wrongly called Basil's 'Rules' are two ascetical works. The first, briefer, one is called the *Little Asceticon* and is preserved only in a Latin translation; the second, more extended, one is called the *Great Asceticon*. In both, the legislator proceeds by questions and answers – conversations between Basil and the monks in the course of his visits. These provide precise directives for everyday life and the organization of a monastic community.

Arles, Museum of Christian Sculpture

A Hymn to God attributed to
Gregory of Nazianzus

You who are beyond all things,
how can we call you by another name?
*   What hymn can we sing to you?*
No word can express you.
*   What spirit can grasp you?*
No mind can conceive of you.
*   You alone are ineffable;*
all that speaks has come forth from you.
*   You alone are unknowable;*
all that thinks has come forth from you.
*   And beings celebrate you,*
those that speak and those that are mute.
*   All beings pay you homage,*
those that think and those that cannot.
*   The universal desire, the groaning of all creation, aspires towards you.*
*   All that exists prays to you*
and towards you all beings that can read your universe
raise a hymn of silence.
*   All that abides, abides in you alone.*
The movement of the universe surges towards you,
*   of all beings you are the goal.*
You are the only one.
*   You are everyone and you are no one.*
You are not a sole being, nor are you the whole:
*   You have every name,*
What can we call you?
*   You are the only one one cannot name:*
what spirit could penetrate the clouds which veil heaven itself?
*   Have pity, you who are beyond all things;*
how can we call you by another name?

The liturgy of Caesarea

Basil's liturgical activity began at Caesarea when he was still a simple priest. He introduced a new form of singing there. He also reformed the liturgical office of the monasteries. The Eastern tradition attributes to him the liturgy which bears his name and which churches of the Byzantine rite still use during Lent and to celebrate great feasts in the year.

Events and responsibilities did not allow Basil to develop his theological genius to the full. His correspondence, one of the most considerable that we have, shows us the daily life of the church, social questions, his sense of friendship and balance, and the strength of character and sensitivity of an incomparable pastor.

2. Gregory of Nazianzus (329–390)

History connects Gregory of Nazianzus closely with his friend Basil, although they were as different as fire and wind. Both came from aristocratic and well-to-do families, and each complements and mutually enriches the other. Gregory's father, who had the same first name as his son, belonged to a Jewish-pagan sect. His wife, who came from a Christian family, exercised a decisive influence on him, which is how he was converted and became Bishop of Nazianzus (present-day Nenizi), to the south-west of Caesarea.

The family put their only son through the classical cycle of studies of the time, rounded off by periods in the great university centres of Constantinople, Alexandria and Athens, where Gregory's friendship with Basil really became established. On his return, around 357, Gregory seems to have received baptism, and then rejoined Basil in his monastic retreat.

Gregory's aging father wanted to appoint his son as successor and ordained him priest against his will (Christmas 361). Gregory did not resist, but then fled, until Easter, when he returned and gave his first sermon, which we still possess.

To increase the voters opposed to the imperial ascendancy, his friend Basil consecrated Gregory Bishop of Sasimus, 'a wretched town' which he was never to visit. Gregory continued to assist his

St Gregory, from a miniature of the *Regula pastoralis* of St Gregory, preserved at Santa Maria Maggiore, Rome

father, and on the latter's death in 374 took over the administration of the diocese of Nazianzus, until a year later he withdrew to a life of solitude at Seleucia, on the coast opposite Cyprus.

It was there that the Christians of Constantinople came in search of him in 379, to make him head of their community, which had been decimated by Arianism but liberated by the death of the emperor Valens. There he gave *Five Theological Discourses* to define the orthodox faith in Christ and in the Trinity. The work is a classic.

He was officially recognized as Bishop of Constantinople by the new emperor, Theodosius, at the Council of Constantinople in 381, but there was a challenge to his nomination from the hierarchy of Egypt and Macedonia, to which Gregory took exception. He left the ecumenical gathering after giving a famous farewell speech, and returned to administer the diocese of Nazianzus for a further two years. Finally, he withdrew to his family estate at Anianzum, where henceforth he was able to devote himself to his literary work until he died in 390.

The theologian

Gregory is the only ancient writer to bear the title of theologian. He owes it above all to his five so-called 'theological' discourses, because they have God as their subject. In them he formulates belief in the Trinity with a depth of expression and a precision of dogmatic formulation which are peculiar to him: 'The proper name of the one who is without origin is the Father; the proper name of the one who is begotten without beginning is the Son; the name of the one who proceeds or comes without being begotten is the Holy Spirit' (*Discourse* 30.19).

Gregory explains the mystery of Christ with the same clarity: 'He condescends to be one, made of two; two natures meet not in two Sons but in a single Son. The two natures are united without either of the two undergoing the least amputation.' The precision of his formulas met with the approval of the Councils of Ephesus (431) and Chalcedon (451).

The humanist and the poet

Gregory has a contrasting personality: the theologian is at the same time a humanist and a poet. The quality of his education appears in his forty-five *Discourses*, which were read and admired to the point of being studied in schools of rhetoric. In them he makes use of an arsenal of procedures and rhythmic skills which can prove tiring in the long term, but which have been the enchantment of centuries. His *Discourses* were copied, translated into every language, and richly illuminated, as the manuscripts show.

The poetic rhythm of Gregory's prose heralds the poems which he wrote towards the end of his life. His ambition was to create a Christian poetry which could rival secular poetry. He composed dogmatic poems on the great truths of faith. His inspiration is most original in the moral poems, in which he expresses with keen sensibility his quest, his suffering, and the melancholy of old age, tinged with hope.

The most important poem, *On his Life* (1,949 lines long), allows us to enter into the closed garden of a poetry which trembles but is always under the sway of an unfailing faith. The Greek soul recognized itself in Gregory and admired him enthusiastically, imitating him in its liturgical hymns. The poet was able to reconcile art and faith, Hellenism and revelation, in a rediscovery of childhood.

3. Gregory of Nyssa (died 394)

The third son of Basil's family, Gregory, was trained in the schools of Cappadocia (Neocaesarea and then Caesarea) in rhetoric and philosophy. After that, in a state of exhilaration, he was trained by his older brother who had returned from abroad. We do not know when Gregory received baptism, but it was certainly not in his infancy, since even Christian families waited for youth to pass before baptism.

Basil's conversion perhaps made Gregory decide to follow an ecclesiastical career as a reader, but he quickly gave this up to teach rhetoric, doubtless after the abrogation of Julian's school law, which banned Christians from teaching. Did he undergo a crisis? The man is too secretive to tell us. During this period Gregory married Theosebia, a very distinguished woman.

In 371 Basil, as Bishop of Caesarea, called on his brother to write a *Treatise on Virginity*, a plea in which he deploys all the resources of rhetoric and diatribe. The next year Basil forced Gregory's hand by ordaining him bishop of a modest place called Nyssa, west of Caesarea, for the same reason as he had nominated his friend Gregory to Sasimus.

With little talent for government, in Nyssa Gregory came up against opposition from the Arians: in 376 a synod of bishops deposed him. On the death of the Emperor Valens in 378 he was able to return to the city in triumph. The next year Gregory lost his sister Macrina and his brother Basil.

A new stage began. For a while Gregory administered the see of Sebaste; he played a prominent role at the Council of Constantinople, became a trusted man at court charged with various missions to Arabia and Jerusalem, and gave funeral orations for

Pulcheria, the emperor's daughter, and the Empress Flavilla. Then, until his death in 394, he devoted himself to literary and theological work. He proved one of the most vigorous of theologians.

Hardly any writer of the first centuries, a period that has not received full recognition, has experienced a revival comparable to that of Gregory of Nyssa. Like the two other Cappadocians he was an admirer of Origen, and seems to have suffered more than them from the later measures taken against that famous Alexandrian theologian. However, Gregory was able to keep his distance. Rather than list his works, it is better to bring out their basic features.

An educator in the faith

Gregory begins by protecting faith from deviations, whether these are the radical Arianism of Eunomius, already contested by his brother, or the Apollinarian error, which mutilated the authentic human nature of Christ in the opposite direction.

The *Catechesis of the Faith*, also called the *Catechetical Discourse*, is a model of the pastoral adaptation of catechesis to a cultivated milieu, nourished by Greek philosophy. With psychological subtlety, here the Bishop of Nyssa addresses catechists, explaining to them not so much the facts of faith as how to make acceptable and accessible to a Greek spirit the truths which are problematical: human nature, the problem of evil, the mystery of the God-man, the drama of his existence which unfolds in the resurrection, the progressive transfiguration of humanity recreated by grace, which makes us artificers of our resemblance to God, and the universal recapitulation of all creation in the final phase. This is an eschatological vision to which Gregory returns several times, principally in his dialogue entitled *Macrina*, or *On the Soul and the Resurrection*.

The reader of scripture

Scripture is the fundamental point of reference for the Bishop of Nyssa. It is not that he multiplies quotations from it, like Augustine, but that he is steeped in it, lives in its world. If he wants to explain the Christian life to the faithful, he gives them a commentary on Ecclesiastes, the Beatitudes, the Our Father.

When Gregory seeks to penetrate the human enigma, he does not interrogate the philosophers but the book of Genesis. When he wants to describe the ways of the mystical life, he uses the book of Exodus, as in the *Life of Moses*, or comments on the Song of Songs.

The various biblical themes – Exodus, Psalms, Ecclesiastes, the Song of Songs – always mark out for him the spiritual way which, through purifications, leads to the inaccessible mystery of God.

The theologian of monasticism and the mystical life

As we have seen, during his lifetime Basil involved his brother in his monastic work. Strangely, he asked Gregory to write a *Treatise on Virginity* when he was still a lay person and married. If in this work Gregory resorts to rhetoric and to commonplaces of the second sophistry, he already shows a very sure feeling for theology and illuminates virginity in the light of creation, in the image and likeness of God.

God is the archetype of virginity, since he engenders without passion. So it is the mystery of the Trinity which gives virginity its foundation and its significance: 'It is in fact an inner and spiritual marriage with God' (*On Virginity*, 20.1).

On the death of Basil, Gregory became his spiritual heir for monasticism. The *Life of Macrina* seeks to present the model of the perfect nun who has attained 'the highest summit of human virtue'. Her biography has the sole aim of showing the route to perfection in a human face, a way which combines culture and holiness, balance and heroism.

It is the same with three other works. There is the *Life of Moses*, 'a treatise on perfection, on the subject of virtue', written at the request of the monk Cesarius. Then there are *Homilies on the Song of Songs*, preached to the community of the famous Olympias, with whom John Chrysostom corresponded. The work describes the spiritual ascension of the soul, intoxicated with the love of God, which 'goes from beginnings to beginnings, by beginnings which have no end'. Finally, Gregory's last

Seeing the Invisible

When we look down from the sublime words of the Lord into the ineffable depths of his thoughts, we have an experience like that of someone gazing from a lofty promontory over the immense sea below.

On the coast one can often see rocky cliffs, the seaward face of which is cut off straight from top to bottom, while their projecting summit forms a peak overhanging the depths. If anyone looked down from such a high peak into the sea below, they would feel giddy. So my soul does now, as it is raised up by this mighty word of the Lord, 'Blessed are the pure in heart, for they shall see God.'

God offers himself to the vision of those who have a pure heart. Now 'no one has ever seen God', as St John says. And St Paul confirms this idea when he speaks of the one 'whom no man has seen or can see'. God is this steep and slippery rock which does not afford the slightest hold for our imagination. Moses, too, in his laws said that God was inaccessible, thus discouraging any attempt to approach him, and his threats explicitly forbid us to seek him: 'No man,' he said, 'can see the Lord and live.'

To see the Lord is eternal life, and yet those pillars of the faith, John and Paul and Moses, declare it to be impossible. What vertigo that causes! Confronted with the abyss of these words, I feel myself fail.

The Lord does not say that it is our joy to see God, but to possess God within ourselves. I do not think that God presents himself face to face to those who have been purified. Perhaps this marvellous saying may suggest what another saying expresses more clearly: 'The kingdom of God is within you.' By this we learn that if our hearts have been purified from every creature and every carnal sentiment, we will see the image of the divine nature in our own beauty. In this brief formula the Word makes a great appeal: 'There is a desire among you human beings to contemplate the true good. When you hear that the majesty of God is enthroned above the heavens, that his glory is inexpressible, his beauty ineffable and his nature inaccessible, do not despair of ever beholding what you desire.' It is indeed within your reach. You have within yourselves a certain aptitude for seeing God; the one who made you at the same time endowed your nature with this marvellous quality. For God imprinted on it the likeness of the glories of his own nature, as if moulding the form of carving into wax. But sin has distorted the imprint of God and this good has become profitless, hidden under a covering of filth. Will you wash off by a good life the stain that has sullied your heart? If you do, your divine beauty will again shine forth in you.

Gregory of Nyssa, *Sermon 6 on the Beatitudes*

work, the *Hypotyposis* (model, example) is a treatise on the monastic life which describes the spiritual journey of the monk and the right use of communal life. It seeks to encourage mystical life in cenobitism, in the tradition of Basil.

Like the other Cappadocians, Gregory is a disciple of Origen, with freedom and a critical sense. Less lyrical than Gregory of Nazianzus, less a statesman than his brother Basil, who at times seems to be rather complicated, Gregory of Nyssa is attractive for the richness of his thought and the vigour of his mind, which is both subtle and penetrating. Mysticism is the natural bent of his theological reflection. Paradox, which scholars call oxymoron (e.g. 'sober drunkenness', 'vigilant sleep', 'luminous darkness', perfection 'the limit of which is not to have any'), perfectly expresses the direction of his spirit.

The chief merit of the Bishop of Nyssa is that he combined theological research with experience in the church and spiritual experience. An incomparable master of mystical theology, he exercised his influence directly and indirectly, in both East and West. Among the Greek writers of the fourth century he is indubitably one of the most distinguished.

VII · Christian Antioch

Antioch, watered by the Orontes, encircled by mountains, capital of Syria, was famous for its monuments. The third city of the empire, it was adorned by the Romans with avenues flanked by statues, with temples, theatres, baths and a stadium. It was there that the disciples of Christ were called Christians for the first time. The community could count famous names among its bishops: Ignatius, Theophilus, Serapion. The historian Eusebius provides us with a list.

It had numerous martyrs, and this led to a great increase in places of pilgrimage. The persecution of Diocletian was particularly trying. Once again it produced a long list of martyrs: priests, women and virgins. John Chrysostom said that the city was encircled with the relics of martyrs as though by a rampart. At the beginning of the fourth century Eustathius, the bishop of the city, was one of the outspoken defenders of the faith of Nicaea.

The Jewish–Christian origins of the community left their mark on the exegesis and theological teaching of the church. It was more a method than a school. The founders seem to have been the priests Dorotheus and Lucian, both martyrs.

The first brilliant teacher in Antioch was Diodore of Tarsus. An exegete by profession, he had written commentaries on all the books of the Bible. We have only fragments of his works. He was clearly the chief thinker in Antioch, a contemporary of the Cappadocians, respected for the quality of his teaching and the austerity of his life. His disciples included John Chrysostom and Theodore of Mopsuestia.

Unlike the Alexandrian, the Antiochian method primarily held to the literal and historical sense of the text, illuminated by its context, and resorted to philology and semantics. In some cases it allowed the typological meaning, based on relations between the two Testaments, alongside the literal meaning, but it proved allergic to Alexandrian allegory.

In fact we find here two complementary approaches, which could have gained by being harmonized. The quarrels and rivalries between sees were to prevent dialogue, provoke excesses of language on both sides and introduce into the debate elements ill-befitting theological research. The dramatic story of John Chrysostom is an illustration.

1. John Chrysostom (died 407)

John was born almost certainly around 349, of a noble family. He lost his father at an early age and was brought up by his mother Anthousa, who was a very religious woman. In all probability the young man became the pupil of the famous sophist Libanius, the glory of Antioch. He received baptism in 368, renounced the career of an advocate, and went to school with Diodore, devoting himself to exegesis and the ascetic life. He allied himself with Theodore of Mopsuestia, then became reader at the church of Antioch.

Desirous of a more perfect life, John left the city to submit himself to the guidance of an ascetic; for two years he lived a solitary life in a cave. His works *Against the Adversaries of the Monastic Life*, *On Virginity* and *To a Young Widow* probably date from this period.

Exhausted by his penance, John returned to Antioch; there he was ordained deacon in 381, and priest five years later. To prepare for it he wrote *On the Priesthood*, a classic of the church. An exceptionally gifted speaker, he dedicated himself to preaching, and this made his reputation. A large number of his homilies on the Old and New Testaments date from this happy period.

John's fame led him to be called to Constantinople to succeed the lordly patriarch Nectarius. The new bishop was the opposite of his predecessor. Instead of luxury he chose privation; he reformed the clergy, inculcated Christian morals into a still

The Eucharist

So many people now say, 'How I would love to see the body of the Lord, his face, his clothes, his shoes!' But it is him whom you see, you touch, you eat. You want to see his clothes, but he gives himself to you not only to see, but to touch, to eat and to receive within you.

Christ is our food

'Who shall declare the mighty works of the Lord, and cause all his praises to be heard?' What shepherd ever fed his sheep with his own body? And why do I say shepherd? There are often mothers who after the travail of giving birth send out their children to nurses. But Jesus Christ cannot suffer that: he feeds us himself with his own blood, and in every way incorporates us into himself.

Note, my brothers, that Christ was born of our own substance; but, you say, that is nothing to all men, though it concerns all. For if he came to take our nature, that evidently concerns all men. And if he came for all, he also came for each one in particular. So how was it, you say, that everyone did not receive from this coming the fruit that they should have done? This was not of his doing, whose choice it was to do it on behalf of all, but the fault of those who were not willing to receive him. For Jesus Christ unites himself in his mysteries with each of his faithful; he gives them new birth, he feeds them with himself and does not abandon them to others, and in this way he convinces us once again that he really took our flesh.

So let us not be indifferent, having received the marks of so great an honour and love. See how eagerly small children take to the breast, and how vigorously they suck at the nipple! Let us imitate them and approach this table and the nipple of the spiritual cup. Or rather, with even more ardour let us draw out the grace of the Spirit, and let it be our sorrow to be deprived of this nourishment.

The same table

What is offered here does not stem from human power. Jesus Christ who once worked these miracles during the supper is the one who works them now. We occupy the place of his servants; it is he who sanctifies these offerings and transforms them. So let no Judas, no covetous man, be present. If any of you are not his disciples, then depart from here. This table does not welcome people like you. 'I keep the Passover with my disciples.' This is the same table here, and it is no less. For Christ did not create one table and men another, but he also made this one. This is the same room where they were then; it is from here that they went out to the Mount of Olives. For the multitude of the poor are like olive trees planted in the house of the God, dropping there the oil that is profitable for us, that oil which we need to live and which the five virgins had, whereas the others who had not kept watch and forgot so that they perished. Let us furnish ourselves, my brothers, with this oil, and let us go before our Bridegroom with shining lamps.

John Chrysostom, *Homily 82 on Matthew*, 4, 5

paganized society, and attacked the splendour of the court as an insult to the wretchedness of ordinary people. In irritation the Empress Eudoxia plotted his downfall. This she achieved easily, thanks to the complicity of Theophilus of Alexandria, who was all too happy to intervene. He had John deposed by the Synod of the Oak, near Chalcedon, on the basis of false accusations. John was sent into exile for the first time. He was already in Bithynia when a popular revolt led to his recall.

The truce was short-lived. After two months, new incidents took place. The bishop was abducted in the middle of celebrating Easter (404) and then definitively sent into exile, first at Cucusa in Lower Armenia. He was then sent on to the fortress of Arabissos at the eastern end of the Black Sea, but never arrived there; he died exhausted on 14 September 407, saying 'Glory to God for all things'.

The man of scripture

'Devote all your leisure to scripture.' Diodore's disciple did not cease to read, meditate and preach on the Bible. No other ancient writer has left us so many books on the Old and New Testaments. In total they amount to some seven hundred homilies. John is the only father to have commented on all the letters of Paul, his favourite author, whom he never ceased to read and reread.

John wrote commentaries on the Gospels of Matthew and John, but Paul remained his constant reading and his point of reference. He was steeped in Paul's spirit. 'I think,' Isidore of Pelusium asserted, 'that if the divine Paul had wanted to comment on himself in the Attic language, he would not have done so in any way differently from this venerable master, so eminent is his exegesis of the Epistle to the Romans in its life, its beauty and the perfection of its style.'

Far from limiting scripture to the clergy, John affirms that the Christian people has even more need of it than the monks. 'Let each one, on returning home, take the Bible in his hand. Let him meditate on what he has heard, if he wishes to derive lasting benefits from scripture.' And elsewhere: 'So do not seek another master; you possess the word of God. No one else will instruct you like it.'

A disciple of the exegetical school of Alexandria, John, far from minimizing intellectual effort, puts the emphasis on work and study. He gives priority to the literal and historical sense. It is useless, he says, to understand the drum and the psaltery in Psalm 149 as the mortification of the flesh and meditation on heaven (as the allegorists do). This verse tells us 'simply to sing joyously the glory of God'. This does not prevent John from following tradition in seeing a figure of the cross in the sacrifice of Abraham.

The defender of the little ones and the poor

Like Basil and Ambrose, John Chrysostom attacks the social scourges of his time, problems which were also severe in Milan, Carthage, Constantinople and Caesarea. John was not content to live an ascetic life; he showed solidarity with the misery of those left out of things: he criticized the unbridled luxury of the court and the well-to-do, and the cupidity of the rich. 'Mules bear fortunes and Christ dies of hunger before your gate.'

Few pastors discerned more clearly than John that the foundation of social justice and charity lies in the eucharist, in the place of the disinherited.

The Emperor Constantine gives his legions the *labarum*, which bears the famous 'chi-rho' monogram (photograph Bibliothèque Nationale)

'You venerate the altar of the church when the body of Christ descends there. But you neglect the other who is the body of Christ, and remain indifferent to him when he dies of hunger.'

The pastor and educator in the faith

John Chrysostom was celebrated as an orator to the point that the ancient world thought that it could hear the accents of Demosthenes again on the banks of the Orontes. However, far from sacrificing to eloquence, he put it at the service of the gospel and the Christian people. All his life he was an educator in the faith and a moralist in the noblest sense of the term, concerned to inculcate Christian morality and to reform a society whose behaviour remained pagan.

Knowing the twists of the human heart, John adapted his words, depending on the situation. To teachers and parents he expounded the beauty of their role, 'the art of arts', which consisted in

Books in the form of a scroll,
from F. Mazois, *Palais de Scaurus*, p. 292

shaping a being. He coined the saying that the Christian home is 'a little church'. To monks and nuns he showed that virginity is a hard struggle, allowing neither relaxation nor repose. So his work is 'a complete manual of the Christian life'.

If John did not have so good a feeling for government as Basil, or the speculative mind of Gregory of Nyssa, he does seem to have plumbed the human heart more deeply. The greatest orators of Greece are his equals, but he has the ardour of the prophets. History has surnamed him 'Golden Mouth'.

2. Theodore of Mopsuestia (died 428)

History has been severe and doubtless unjust towards John Chrysostom's friend Theodore, the Bishop of Mopsuestia. Like him, Theodore came from Antioch, where he had been the pupil of the sophist Libanius. First a priest, he became Bishop of Mopsuestia in Cilicia in 392. He gained a reputation above all for exegetical skill and orthodoxy. He is considered the greatest of the Antiochene masters.

Since after Theodore's death his work was drawn into the christological dispute, and he became the favourite target of the Monophysites, he ended up being condemned with Diodore at the Council of Constantinople in 553, on the basis of a collection of hostile forged extracts from his works. His works themselves disappeared. Only his *Baptismal Catecheses* have been preserved in a Syriac translation. We have just fragments of his exegetical work, but at least they allow us to appreciate his perfect orthodoxy, the rigour of his method and his moderate use of typology to interpret the Old Testament.

VIII · Gaul and the West Awaken

In the West, only Africa and, thanks to Hippolytus, Rome show any literary and theological vitality during the third century. The map of the Christian West was to change a century later and to present some figureheads: Hilary of Poitiers, Ambrose of Milan and Jerome of Stridon, who prepared the way for the most famous figure of all, Augustine the African, in the wake of Tertullian and Cyprian.

The reconciliation and then the alliance of the Western and Eastern empires dominate the whole history of the fourth and fifth centuries. Because it broke up so quickly, the unity achieved by Constantine, sealed by the new Rome on the Bosphorus, compromised the unity of the church. Dialogue proved increasingly difficult, and East and West went their separate ways, no longer speaking the same language.

For a while, the Western church was colonized culturally by the East. Ambrose and Jerome were still nurtured on Origen. Ambrose introduced chant borrowed from the East. Hilary enriched his thought by contact with Eastern theology and exegesis. Athanasius introduced the vitality of Egyptian and Syrian monasticism to Rome, bringing monks with him to demonstrate it.

Arianism is a typically Eastern product. The controversy which provoked the Council of Nicaea did not disturb any bishops in the West. Hilary acknowledged with candour that he had never heard of the faith of Nicaea before his exile. Without the disastrous intervention of the emperor Constans, in all probability the conflict would have been limited to the East. It was not until the fifth century that with Pelagianism the first theological controversy broke out in Africa, and that left the Christian East indifferent.

Be this as it may, in the fourth century the Christian West not only emerged but asserted itself and assumed a stature of its own. The church of Rome became Latinized, and Italy achieved prominence, above all with Ambrose of Milan, but also with less famous writers like Eusebius of Vercelli, Lucifer of Cagliari, Zeno of Verona and Rufinus of Aquileia; a generation later came Maximus of Turin and Chrysologus of Ravenna.

Gaul made its entry into Christian literature. The obscure city of Poitiers produced a high-flying theologian, and Bordeaux gave birth to the enigmatic poet Ausonius, and Bishop Paulinus who was to settle in Nola. Provence with Marseilles and Lérins became a centre of great vitality, so much so that this disturbed Rome.

Jerome came from Dalmatia and Nicetas from Dacia on the Mediterranean. In the extreme west, the Iberian peninsula made its mark and organized itself. Bishops multiplied and councils met. The famous synod of Elvira was held at the beginning of the fourth century. There were numerous writers: Ossius at Cordova, Potamius at Lisbon, Gregory of Elvira, Pacian of Barcelona, Orosius at Braga. And one might add two authentic poets, Juvencus and Prudentius.

The osmosis between East and West was encouraged, first by the Emperor Constantine and then, after the violent death of Constans, by the conquest of Constantius, who became sole emperor. He constantly put the episcopate under pressure, leading to the Councils of Arles (353) and Milan (355) which called for the condemnation of Athanasius. Recalcitrant churchmen were sent into exile. Peace and orthodoxy returned only with the emperor Theodosius.

1. Gaul and Hilary of Poitiers (died 367)

No writer stands out more in Christian Gaul than Hilary, who appeared for the first time in 356, at the Council of Béziers: on refusing to condemn Athanasius, he was exiled to Phrygia. These years were to prove decisive in the maturing of his theology.

At the beginning of his *Treatise on the Trinity*, Hilary recalls his conversion, describing his inner journey, his quest for God, comparable to that of Justin, which was both philosophical and religious, and the response which came to him from the Bible and the Gospel of John. He ended up becoming bishop of the community.

With his lucid and mature faith, Hilary rapidly saw the theological implications of the emperor's demands. He headed the opposition, defending orthodox faith by instinct, without having heard of the Council of Nicaea. 'I had long been baptized and had been exercising the functions of a bishop for some time, but had never heard mention of the creed of Nicaea, except when I went into exile' (*De Synodis* 20).

Defender of the faith

Hilary is commonly called the Athanasius of the West. This comparison is justified because of the orthodoxy of his doctrine and his theological work. However, this prudent and moderate Gaul did not have the fighting temperament of the Bishop of Alexandria. He was the first theologian on the European continent to make his mark by the originality of his thought and the vigour of his dialectic.

Hilary's main work is his *Treatise on the Trinity*, a work of impressive dimensions which runs to twelve books. It seems as if the author has fused two works into one: a first study of the faith and then a systematic refutation of the theses of Arius, along with the arguments and biblical texts that he uses. Hilary strongly affirms: 'The Son is eternal, always Son, because he is born by a generation outside time which is incomprehensible to us.'

Like all the anti-Arian trend, he did not develop the humanity of Christ to the full. However, by virtue of its exhaustive character and its dimensions, his treatise on the Trinity represents a new development in Latin literature which was to have considerable influence on the Arian debate and on later centuries.

The Bishop of Poitiers methodically collected essential material with a view to a doctrinal history on the Council of Rimini (359), *The Historical Fragments*. The documents which have come down to us are either material collected by Hilary or documents drawn from a larger work composed by him. Scholars generally tend towards the second hypothesis. At any rate, these documents are historical and theological material of the utmost importance.

The pastor and the spiritual master

Two works show us another side to Hilary. The *Treatise on the Mysteries* – rediscovered in a mutilated form in 1887 – seems to have been composed for priests or catechists. It is a Christian re-reading of the Old Testament in which the biblical figures – Adam, Noah, Melchizedek and Abraham – are the prophetic announcements of Christ and the church. This typology was highly traditional in East and West, allowing Old Testament figures and events to be interpreted in the light of the Messiah. Thus Eve is the prefigurement of the universal resurrection.

The other book, the *Commentary on the Psalms*, is more of a spiritual and theological work. It deals with only a selection of Psalms. Composed after his exile, it shows clearly the influence exerted by Origen, whether in the treatment of hermeneutical questions or in allegorical interpretation. Here again, a single reading of the Psalms, as a prophetic proclamation of Christ, from his birth to his glory, makes it possible to penetrate their inner and spiritual meaning.

The prayer of the Psalms, for Hilary as for Ambrose and Augustine, marks the route which leads to the city of God. So Hilary's commentaries relate more to spiritual theology than to exegesis, and describe the quest for God.

The unrecognized liturgist

In more than one commentary on Matthew, also perhaps written for priests, Hilary is the first liturgical author in the West. Unfortunately few of his hymns have come down to us. The example of the East, where poetry was used to spread doctrine, may have inspired the bishop to use this means of dissemination. Hilary's prose was laboured and obscure, and would have had less effect in the West than the more gracious style of Ambrose.

Baptistery of St John, Poitiers

Prayer

O Almighty God the Father, I am fully aware that the first duty that I owe to you is that all my words and thoughts should speak only of you. The gift of speech which I have comes from you. It can obtain for me no greater reward here than to serve you by proclaiming you and revealing to the world that does not know you and the heretic who denies you what you are, namely, the Father of the only begotten Son of God. That is my sole ambition.

For the rest, I pray for your help and mercy that you may fill the sails of our faith and Christian profession with the breath of the Spirit. Speed us on our way, that we may better proclaim your message! He is not unfaithful to your promise who has told us, 'Ask and you shall receive, seek and you shall find, knock and it shall be opened to you.'

So in our poverty we turn towards you; we shall apply ourselves with tireless zeal to the study of all the words of your prophets and apostles and knock on all the doors of wisdom that are closed to us. However, it is for you alone to grant our prayer to be present when we seek, to open when we knock. Because of the laziness and dullness of our nature, we are as it were in a trance, and when we seek to know your nature or your properties, the infirmity of our spirit keeps us restricted within the confines of your ignorance. But the study of your teaching leads us to grasp the knowledge of divine things, and the obedience of faith takes us beyond the resources of our nature.

We have the firm hope that you will inspire the beginnings of this timid venture, that you will encourage it with steady progress, that you will communicate to us the spirit of the prophets and the apostles, so that we can explain the proper meaning of the words in accordance with the realities that they signify. Our plan is to speak of what is expressed in the mystery: that you are the eternal God, the Father of the eternal only-begotten God; and the one Lord Jesus Christ who is born from you for all eternity, without increasing the number of Gods but also without denying that the Christ is born of you, the one God; above all, without seeking to refuse to acknowledge him as the true God, who is born of you, true God and Father of Jesus Christ.

Hilary of Poitiers, *On the Trinity*, I, 37, 38

Profession of Faith

O Holy Father, Omnipotent God, as long as I enjoy the life which you have given me I shall proclaim you as the eternal God and also as the eternal Father. Nor shall I ever express such folly and impiety as to make myself judge of your omnipotence and mysteries, and put the feeble understanding of my weakness above the true notion of your infinity and faith in your eternity. I shall never affirm that you could have existed without your Wisdom, your Virtue, your Word: the only-begotten God, my Lord Jesus Christ.

Since I do not even know myself, I admire you all the more because I am ignorant of myself. Without comprehending it, I perceive the mechanism of my reason and the life of my spirit; and I owe this experience to you, since you grant me something beyond the understanding of principles, namely the understanding of the nature that fills me with delight.

And since I know you, though I am ignorant of myself, if my knowledge turns to worship, I shall not lessen my belief in your omnipotence because it is so much above me. So I cannot claim to be able to conceive of the origin of your only-begotten Son: to do that would be to want to become the judge of my Creator and my God.

Keep intact, I pray you, this piety of my faith, and to the end of my life give me this awareness of my knowledge, that I may hold fast to what I possess, what I professed in the creed of my regeneration when I was baptized in the name of the Father, and of the Son, and of the Holy Spirit.

Grant that I may adore you, our Father, and your Son together with you, and that I may be worthy of the Holy Spirit who proceeds from you through the only Son. He bears witness to my faith who says, 'Father, all things that are mine are yours, and yours are mine' – my Lord Jesus Christ, who for ever abides as God in you, from you and with you, who is blessed for ever and ever. Amen.

Hilary of Poitiers, *On the Trinity*, XIII, 52, 53, 57

2. Ambrose of Milan, the accomplished pastor (337/9–397)

In moving from Hilary to Ambrose we leave Gaul for Italy. The two men were confronted with different situations, even if both were involved in the church's Arian crisis in different ways.

Ambrose was a patrician born in Trier in 337 or 339, when his father was there as administrator of the prefecture of Gaul. On the latter's death, the family returned to Rome, where the young man devoted himself to study, and became first an advocate and then consular prefect of Emilia, with his residence in Milan.

Auxentius, the bishop of the city, was an unrepentant Arian, and that divided the community. The election of a successor proved to be turbulent and difficult, so the prefect was present to ensure order and impartiality. Of one accord, Arians and catholics both acclaimed Ambrose bishop, though he was only a catechumen. He received baptism and then, eight days later, episcopal ordination, almost certainly on 7 December 374. He then distributed all his goods to the poor and the church.

His first task was to apply himself to gaining a deep knowledge of scripture, drawing on the exegesis of Philo and above all Origen. This task was made easy by his fluency in Greek. Meditation and prayer brought his theological training to maturity and prepared him for his pastoral activity.

From his past, the bishop preserved a feeling for government and its responsibilities, an innate authority which forced the imperial power to bend, beginning with the Empress Justin, the protector of the Aryans. Ambrose's aim was to liquidate Arianism south of the Alps. He intervened in the election of bishops, like that of the Bishop of Sirmium, whose orthodoxy he knew. After that he used his influence on emperors from Valentinian I to Gratian in order to defeat the last counter-offensives of Arianism.

Relations with Valentinian II were alternately

St Ambrose refusing the Emperor Theodosius admittance to the church (engraving by
S. Freeman after Vandyck, Hulton Deutsch)

difficult and peaceful. For example, the massacre of the population of Thessalonica by the emperor led to extreme tension. The bishop called for public penance, which Valentinian performed at Christmas 390. Harmony was re-established, and Ambrose gave the emperor's funeral oration in the presence of Honorius.

The influence of the Bishop of Milan on the emperor then diminished. He devoted his time to the internal life of the church, intensified the cult of martyrs, discovered the remains of Nazarius and Celsus (having earlier discovered those of the proto-martyrs of Milan, Gervasius and Protasius), created new sees and nominated their bishops. He died in Milan on 4 April 397.

Mosaic of St Ambrose, Milan

Profile

A mosaic in Milan from less than a century after his death depicts Ambrose as being short, emaciated, bearded with a long sloping face, with a meditative expression and two dark eyes expressing authority and contemplation, a controlled fervour and a shyness which puts one at a distance.

Ambrose could doubtless have governed the empire as easily as the church. A complete man, with amazing gifts, he was both active and contem-

plative, an intellectual and an orator, who won over Augustine and beat him on his own ground; always able to cope with the most difficult situations and tasks without any effort. Such was Bishop Ambrose.

His writings which have come down to us show the various aspects of his work: theological, social, political, pastoral and spiritual.

A man of scripture

Like Cyprian before him and Augustine after him, Ambrose was first of all trained in the school of the Bible, the book which never again left his side. The Bible remained the object of his spiritual meditation and the source of his preaching to the people. The majority of his exegetical writings derive from sermons which were later written to extend his pastoral work. If he wanted to deal with a question like evil, the soul, death, riches, by preference he would begin from a biblical figure. Jacob allowed him to expand on a happy life, Elijah on fasting.

Steeped in the Jewish exegesis of Philo and above all the Christian exegesis of Origen, the bishop developed the three-fold sense of scripture – literal, moral, and allegorical/spiritual – while remaining constantly attentive to the typology which harmonizes the two Testaments.

When Ambrose preached on scripture, he raised burning questions: the doctrinal deviations of the Arians, the errors of the Manichaeans or the Sabellians, and even more the vices and the flaws of the age: avarice, drunkenness and gluttony. His constant concern was to Christianize the community.

Ambrose wrote a commentary on the Gospel of Luke, perhaps to imitate Origen, but doubtless also because with all his spiritual sensitivity he was attuned to the themes of mercy, and concern for women and the poor. Like Hilary he sought a way towards encounter with God in the prayer of the Psalms. Death surprised him while he was writing a commentary on Psalm 43.

At the service of the liturgy

This pastor was at the same time a liturgist, who has left us two versions of the baptismal and mystagogical catechesis. These enrich our knowledge of the liturgy in Milan. To the alternate chanting of psalms he added an innovation, hymns, which from now on were to flourish in Milan. Though he himself did compose hymns, many texts attributed to him are spurious. He is considered the founder of liturgical hymnology in the West.

For the training of the emperor Gratian, Ambrose composed dogmatic treatises on faith, the Holy Spirit and the Incarnation. These allowed the emperor to follow theological debates more clearly.

The advocate of the poor and weak

The social and economic situation in Milan was like that in Caesarea or Constantinople. The small folk were oppressed by taxation and the power of the rich. The aristocrat who had given his fortune to the poor now lent them his words and his actions. He pleaded their cause in his *The Story of Naboth* with the rigour of a lawyer and the heart of a pastor. Rarely has a Christian text taught with such force the just sharing of possessions which belong to all, the law and also the limits of property.

The spiritual guide

Aware of his pastoral responsibility, Ambrose was first of all concerned about the quality of his clergy. After the rout of Arianism, he took great care not to profit from the situation by taking drastic measures. He composed a code of life, *The Duties of Ministers*, primarily for the clergy but not forgetting the Christian people.

The bishop was above all concerned for Christian women – virgins, widows, nuns – and wrote a great many works on them, for the most part deriving from homilies addressed to them. His correspondence extended his pastoral work. He wrote a treatise *On Virginity* for his sister Marcellina, who had become a nun.

Events, mourning, the loss of a brother, the passing of the days provided the bishop with occasions for meditating on death. As well as his funeral orations, he wrote two treatises on the topic: *Death is a Blessing* and a masterpiece, *The Happy Life*. In them we find the confidence of a warm sensitivity and the vigour of a hope stronger than death.

Naboth the Poor

You yourself permanently benefit when you give to the poor. That of which you deprive yourself accrues to you. You nourish yourself with food even when you offer to the poor, since the one who has pity on the poor refreshes himself precisely in so doing, and tastes the fruit inherent in his works. Mercy is sown on earth, and has its origin in the skies. It is planted in the poor and blossoms abundantly in God. Do not say 'I commend you to God, I will give you something tomorrow.' How could the one who cannot bear your saying 'I will give you something tomorrow' suffer your saying, 'I will not give you anything'?

Besides, it is not from your own goods that you distribute to the poor; you are simply giving him what is his. For you have simply usurped what is given to all for the use of all. The earth belongs to all and not to the rich, but those who do not make use of their possessions are more numerous than those who do. Thus, far from making free gifts, you are paying your debt.

You clothe your walls and you denude human beings. The poor man who is naked cries in front of your house and you neglect him. He cries, and your sole concern is to decide what kind of marble you want to use for your pavements. The poor man asks for money and does not get it. He asks for bread, and your horse champs on its golden bit. Costly jewels are your delight, while others have no grain. What a terrible judgment you bring down on yourselves, you rich! The people are dying of hunger and you barricade the granaries; they weep in misery and you hurl rocks at them! Unhappy man, you have the power to snatch so many people from death, but you have no will to do so. The precious stone which gleams in your ring could save the life of a whole people.

You are the gaoler of your goods and not their sovereign, you who bury your gold in the earth, you who are its servants and not its masters. 'But where your treasure is, there your heart is also.' And this gold is your heart which you have buried. Go, sell your gold and buy salvation; sell minerals and acquire the kingdom of God; sell the field and buy eternal life.

Ambrose, *The Story of Naboth*

3. The other writers of Italy

Italian theology was not limited to Ambrose. The bishop of Milan was surrounded by a galaxy of writers who are known to us by their works: Zeno, Chromatius and Rufinus, who was first a friend and then an opponent of Jerome, and one of the translators of the Greek heritage.

In the middle of the fourth century, probably at Rome, an anonymous author whom scholars have still not been able to identify composed a *Commentary on the Letters of St Paul* which in the Middle Ages was attributed to St Ambrose. It is an original work which provides a commentary of a literary and historical kind, along Antiochene lines.

A generation later we find two bishops who have left us some very fine sermons: Maximus of Turin (died 408/423) and Peter Chrysologus, Bishop of Ravenna (died 450).

4. Jerome of Stridon, monk and exegete (347–420)

Jerome is difficult to place. A Dalmatian, he opted for Latin culture: a man of the West, he spent the greater part of his life in the East, settling in Bethlehem for his biblical studies more than out of sympathy with the Eastern world.

He was born at Stridon, an unidentified place on the frontier between the Latin world and Pannonia. His well-to-do Christian family saw that he had an extremely thorough education. He did all his studies in Rome, in addition leading a life of pleasure, interspersed with moments of devotion. In Rome he decided to receive baptism before leaving for Trier.

Jerome's desire for the monastic life led him to stay with friends in Aquileia. He then left for a first visit to the East, to live in the desert of Chalcis in Syria (375–377). Eventually he quarrelled with the monks and went to Antioch; though he questioned the exegesis there he was later to take it up. From Antioch he went to Constantinople where he met Gregory of Nazianzus, who made him enthusiastic about Origen.

After Gregory's departure, Jerome left the city and returned to Rome the long way round. There he became the confidant of the octogenarian pope Damasus, allied himself with the well-to-do ladies of the Aventine whom he filled with enthusiasm for biblical studies, and began a revision of the Latin text of the four Gospels.

On the death of his protector Damasus, feeling the hostility of the clergy, Jerome left Rome for the East, and finally settled in Bethlehem; he was accompanied by rich matrons, whose immense fortune was to finance his study and his work. He died in 420.

Jerome the man is even more complicated than his life is turbulent. He is both rude and sensitive; refined in the writing of his letters and unsystematic in his translations, which are sometimes slapdash; and incapable of controlling his passion, which led him to the point of being vindictive and unjust.

For history, Jerome is the man of the Bible. In this capacity, among the Latins he became the precursor of the humanists of the Renaissance. However, he can also be given other titles.

The man of letters

The most well-groomed part of Jerome's work is his correspondence. More than in any other writing, at this point the style is in the image of the man, refined to the point of preciousness, a mixture of excess and delicacy. Jerome exercised a real epistolary apostolate, directing devout women, enlightening Nepotian on the duties of the clergy, and treating in turn virginity, widowhood, the monastic life, the education of young women, and biblical questions. Here we also find praise for his feminine disciples.

The witness of monasticism

Despite the faults which he could not disguise, Jerome was a monk at heart. He was a true son of Antony, whose life doubtless prompted his vocation. Despite his restless existence and his frequent disputes with the monks of the East, he never trifled with the rigours of asceticism, which he practised up to his death.

Knowing the Bible

There is a 'wisdom of God in a mystery, even the hidden wisdom, which God ordained before the world' (I Cor. 2.7). God's wisdom is Christ, for Christ, we are told, is 'the power of God and the wisdom of God' (cf. I Cor. 1.30).

This wisdom remains hidden in a mystery. It is to this that the title of Ps. 9.1, 'for the hidden things of the son' (Ps. 9.1), alludes. In him are hidden all the treasures of wisdom and knowledge (cf. Col. 2.3). He also who was hidden in a mystery is the same that was foreordained before the world, foreordained and prefigured in the Law and the Prophets. That is why the prophets were called seers: they saw him whom others did not see. Abraham also saw his day, and was glad (cf. John 8.56). The heavens which were sealed to a rebellious people were opened to Ezekiel (1.1). 'Open my eyes,' says David, 'that I may behold the wondrous things of your law' (Ps. 118.18). For the law is spiritual, and in order to understand it we need the veil to be removed and the glory of God to be seen with face uncovered (cf. II Cor. 3.14–18).

In the Apocalypse a book is shown sealed with seven seals. If you give it to someone who is learned, saying 'Read this,' he will reply, 'I cannot, for it is sealed.' How many people are there today who think themselves to be learned, yet the scriptures are a sealed book to them! And they are incapable of opening it except through him who has the key of David: 'he opens and no one shuts; he shuts and no one opens' (Rev. 3.7).

In the Acts of the Apostles, the holy eunuch (or rather man, for that is what scripture calls him) is asked by Philip while reading Isaiah, 'Do you understand what you are reading?' 'How can I,' he replies, 'unless someone teaches me?' (Acts 8.30–31). I am no more holy nor more diligent than this eunuch. He came from Ethiopia, that is from the ends of the world; leaving a royal court he went as far as the Temple; and such was his zeal for the knowledge of God that even on his chariot he was reading the holy scriptures. Yet although he held the book in his hand and was reflecting on the words of the Lord, even articulating them with his tongue and pronouncing them with his lips, he did not know the one whom, still without knowing it, he was worshipping in this book. Then Philip came along: he showed him Jesus hidden under the letter. What marvellous power of the teacher! In the same hour the eunuch believed and was baptized; he became one of the faithful and a saint. He was no longer a pupil but a master; and he found more in the desert spring of the church than he had done in the gilded temple of the synagogue.

I have summed up all this briefly; I could not do more than this within the confines of a letter. But you should understand that you cannot make any progress in the Holy Scriptures unless you have a guide to show you the way.

I beg of you, my dearest brother, to live among these sacred books, to meditate upon them ceaselessly, to know nothing else, to seek nothing else. Does not such a life seem to you to be a foretaste of heaven here on earth? Do not let the simplicity of Holy Scripture or the poorness of its vocabulary offend you; for these are due either to the faults of translators or else even serve some purpose. For it thus offers itself in such a way that an uneducated congregation can find some benefit there and the scholar and the unlettered can discover unexpected meanings in one and the same sentence. I am not so dull nor so forward as to claim that I know all that is in Scripture; to do that would be to want to pluck on earth the fruits of trees whose roots are in heaven. However, I confess that I would like to do so. So let us study here on earth that knowledge which will continue with us in heaven.

Jerome, *Letter* 53, 4, 5, 6, 10

Jerome to Augustine

Far be it from me to presume to attack anything that your Grace has written. For it is enough for me to prove my own views without criticizing those that others hold. But it is well known to one of your wisdom that everyone is satisfied with his own opinion, and that it is puerile self-sufficiency to seek, as has long been the wont of young men, to gain glory for one's own name by attacking those who have become famous. I am not so foolish as to feel insulted by the fact that you give different explanations from mine; nor should you be, if my views are contrary to those which you hold. What is truly reprehensible among friends is when each, not seeing his own bag of faults, looks deep into the wallet the other carries, as Persius puts it. Let me add: love one who loves you, and as a young man do not challenge a veteran in the field of scripture. I have had my time, and have run my course to the utmost of my strength. It is only fair that I should rest and that you in turn should run and cover great distances.

Jerome, *Letter* 102.2

To exalt monasticism, Jerome wrote biographical novels on Paul of Thebes, Hilarion of Gaza and Malchus, in the style later made popular by the Golden Legend. At the end of his life he propagated the writings of Pachomian circles.

The fighter

Jerome spent his life fighting, often for legitimate causes but with means hardly in keeping with the gospel. It was not good to have him as an enemy. His portraits of Roman clergy have a ferocity which is intensified by the elegance of his style.

His often unjustified changes of mind made his friends the butt of his sarcasms or his pamphlets. He owed everything to Origen, but did not forgive him his superiority, and persecuted him after ransacking his works. He parted company with his friend Rufinus out of rivalry and persecuted him after his death.

His taste for polemic led Jerome, like Tertullian, to write work after work beginning with 'Against', sometimes involving himself in conflicts with a bear-like clumsiness. He fanned the flames of the Pelagian controversy.

The translator of the Eastern heritage

Leaving scripture aside, Jerome, who had become familiar with Greek while in the East, first translated the writings of Eusebius, which gave him tools for his work: the *Chronicles*, and the *Onomasticon*, a dictionary of biblical sites. Even his book of *Illustrious Men* merely capitalizes on Eusebius's *Church History*, adding to it a notice about himself.

In his youth Jerome translated Origen's homilies, not without an ulterior motive (he wanted to show Ambrose up as a plagiarist); the same goes for his translation of the *Treatise on the Holy Spirit* by Didymus the Blind.

The exegete and textual critic

Jerome's greatest work is in the field of exegesis. A man of the Bible, first in the traditional line of typology and allegory, like Origen and Hilary before him and Augustine after him he gradually came closer to the Antiochene tradition which favoured the literal sense, familiarizing himself with Greek and Hebrew. This allowed him to read and translate from the original. His task was greatly facilitated by the Origen library, which he could consult in Caesarea. He was heavily dependent on the Hexapla. It would not be unfair to apply to him the saying he pinned on Ambrose: 'A jay decked in peacock's feathers'.

The great period of Jerome's translations is between 391 and 406, when he retranslated the books of the Old Testament from the original and established the basis of the Latin Bible, called the Vulgate. He was far from careful and attentive, as he is in his letters, but worked quickly, to the point of translating Proverbs, Ecclesiastes and the Song of Songs in three days.

He devoted the last part of his life to commentaries, in the widest sense of the term. He commented verse by verse on the letters of Paul (which he did not have in Latin) in order to explain them. In this way he wanted to introduce his spiritual daughters in Bethlehem to scripture.

From Paul, Jerome went on to the Old Testament: first Ecclesiastes, then the Psalms, and finally the prophets, his masterpiece. He moved from the minor prophets to the great prophets: Daniel (407),

Isaiah (408–410), Ezekiel (411–414). His work on Jeremiah remained unfinished since he had reached the end of his life.

Jerome's method is very clear: he establishes the text from the Hebrew and translates it, gives a literal commentary, and then a spiritual commentary. Despite his faults (his digressions and his short-sightedness), Jerome occupies a unique place in the Latin church, as an exegete.

IX · The Blossoming of Latin Poetry from Damasus to Sedulius

We have already come across two poets, known more for their prose: Hilary of Poitiers and Ambrose of Milan. Those who followed in the fourth and fifth centuries were from different backgrounds: Damasus and Prudentius from Spain, Ausonius and Paulinus from Gaul, Sedulius perhaps from Rome.

Poetry lagged behind prose, though that being said a qualification must be added. We have to take account of the fact that from the beginning the liturgy used 'psalms, hymns and spiritual songs', of which the New Testament writings and the East have preserved some specimens. We might remember the Odes of Solomon and the songs used by the heretics in East and West for propaganda. The hymns of the time had no literary pretensions.

Both poetry and the vocabulary used by pagan religion appeared when Christianity triumphed; hitherto it had been immunized against the seductions of paganism. In the fourth century poetry allied technique with creativity. A variety of names appear, including Juvencus of Gaul and Ausonius of Bordeaux, a prisoner of paganism who remained half-way between his culture and Christianity.

1. Pope Damasus (died 384)

We have already met Damasus in connection with the life of Jerome. He was born in Rome but seems to have been of Spanish origin. He succeeded the unfortunate Pope Liberius, who was ignominiously exiled by Constantius in the Arian crisis. Around the middle of the fourth century the Roman liturgy changed from Greek to Latin.

Little suited to theological controversy, which, as Basil put it, he treated lightly, Damasus had a predilection for the muses. His pontificate coincided with the blossoming of liturgical architecture and the cult of martyrs, which brought floods of pilgrims to Rome. The poet enjoyed composing epigrams in hexameters, which were engraved in elegant uncials by Philoculus to adorn the tombs of the martyrs. One of them has been restored at St Clement in Rome. It represents minor versifying, of more archaeological than literary interest.

2. Prudentius the Spaniard (died after 405)

The career of the Spaniard Aurelius Prudentius was quite different. He came from a cultured Christian family in Calahorra, Northern Spain, and first of all underwent the *cursus honorum*. He was made prefect and governor of important cities. An inner crisis put an end to his secular life. Prudentius took up the life of a recluse, albeit a comfortable one, in order to celebrate God through poetry, which for him served as a domestic liturgy.

Of his various works (including *The Book of Crowns* and *The Battle of the Soul*), the one which made the most impression on subsequent generations and even on the Roman liturgy was the Book of Hours (*Kathemerinon*); in this he celebrated the hours and the days, including the most popular days in the liturgy, Christmas and Epiphany.

Prudentius' poetry is close to that of Ambrose, but it has no liturgical pretensions and is less structured. It is also distinct from that of Hilary, which is more strongly theological. At the end of his life, the poet sought to express his Christian profession in thanksgiving and praise.

3. Paulinus of Bordeaux, Bishop of Nola (353/4–431)

Paulinus was born in Bordeaux of a senatorial family, which had vast estates. He became the pupil of Ausonius, a refined poet, to whom he remained attached and with whom he exchanged writings. He came to Rome to succeed his father in the senate and then became governor of Campania.

On his return to Gaul, Paulinus married. In 389 he was baptized in Bordeaux and five years later ordained priest. He resolved to give away all his possessions and live a monastic life, settling by the tomb of St Felix at Nola. His wife went into a monastery. The city elected Paulinus bishop, somewhere between 409 and 413.

Apart from his correspondence, which put him in touch with various important figures of the period, friends, writers and bishops (including Jerome and Augustine), Paulinus left a collection of twenty-nine poems. He dabbled in poetry for many occasions: the death of a child; the marriage of a friend, Julian, who was to be Bishop of Eclanum; and the visit of Bishop Nicetas.

Fourteen songs composed between 395 and 408 celebrate the anniversaries of St Felix. They describe the crowds which thronged in, the naive demonstrations of popular piety, and the miracles performed. Here imagination takes the place of historical rigour. Less brilliant and less sparkling above all than that of Prudentius, the poetry of Paulinus resembles the man, radiating freshness, charm and sensitivity. Moreover it is of authentically Christian inspiration.

4. Sedulius (died 420–430)

The poet Sedulius, who was also a priest, seems to have put his art at the service of liturgical celebration. His *Paschal Chant* is a poetical catechesis which seeks to hymn the marvels of the God of the Old

---

Prudentius: Hymn for the Holy Innocents

Alarmed, the impious tyrant hears
That now the King of Kings has come
To sit on David's royal throne
And rule the race of Israel.

And maddened by the news, he cries,
'This upstart comes to banish me:
Go warriors, unsheathe your swords,
And stain the infants' cribs with blood.'

Of what avail such wickedness?
What joy in crime does Herod find?
Alone among so many slain,
Unharmed and safe, the Christ child lives.

All hail, sweet flowers of martyrdom,
Cut down in life's bright dawning hour,
And shattered by the foe of Christ
As rosebuds by the whirling storm.

First victims offered up to Christ,
A tender flock of spotless lambs,
Before God's very altar throne,
With martyrs' crowns and palms you play.

from Sister H. Clement Eagan, *The Poems of Prudentius*, Washington DC 1962, 88f.

---

and New Testaments. Several other hymns passed into the liturgy for the festivals of Christmas and Epiphany. One text was even used – uniquely – as an introit to the mass.

Sedulius was very popular in the Middle Ages. His works can be found in all the monastic libraries. The Renaissance and Luther himself called Sedulius 'the most Christian of the poets'.

Baptistery of Manosque, Provence
(photograph Roger-Viollet)

X · The Glory of the West: Augustine the African (354–430)

Augustine, a product of Romanized Africa, is the last of the great writers in Latin. In him all the riches of his contemporaries seem to be concentrated. The life of this African orator, closely bound up with the history of the late empire, begins to take on apocalyptic colours as this history does. Augustine witnessed the fall of Rome and died in a city besieged by the Vandals.

He was born in the south of consular Africa at Thagaste, present-day Souk-Ahras, in Algeria. His father, the owner of a small estate, was a pagan, and his mother, Monica, a fervent Christian. Augustine first went to school at Thagaste, continued his studies at Madaura, and, through the generosity of a patron, finished them at Carthage, where 'a cauldron of illicit loves hissed around me'.

The death of his father forced Augustine to return home to support his family. He taught first at Thagaste, then at Carthage and in Rome, finally occupying a prebendal chair in Milan. There he decided to be baptized (23 April 387). It is in this event that his *Confessions* culminate.

After the death of his mother at Ostia, Augustine finally left Italy with some friends and his son Adeodatus, to live a monastic life at Thagaste. There he devoted himself to asceticism and study, and waited for the sign from heaven which, when it came, was not what he had expected. In 391, restless and seeking a place to found a monastery, he moved to the busy sea port of Hippo.

1. Augustine, Bishop of Hippo

On arriving in Hippo, to his surprise he was chosen as priest. He accepted on condition that he could have a year to prepare for his ministry. In 396 he succeeded the old bishop at the head of the second diocese in Africa, where he remained until his death.

From now on, his actions and work were closely linked. Little by little the bishop became established as the most noted authority in the Christian West, the conscience of the church.

2. The theological controversies

Like those who rebuilt Jerusalem after the exile, Augustine worked with trowel and sword. Three controversies shook Africa: Manichaeanism, Donatism and Pelagianism.

Manichaeanism seduced Augustine for a while. Heir to Gnosticism, Manichaeanism professed a radical dualism in which the principle of light was opposed by the evil principle in a merciless struggle. This was one way of explaining evil. Augustine

---

Take, Read!

I was asking myself these questions, and weeping all the time with the bitterest sorrow in my heart. All at once I heard a voice coming from a nearby house. I do not know whether it was that of a boy or a young girl, but again and again it kept repeating, 'Take, read! Take, read!' I looked up, and wondered whether there was any kind of game in which children used a refrain like this, but nothing came to mind. Suppressing the violence of my tears I got up; the only interpretation I could put on it was that this was a divine command bidding me open the book of scripture and read the first chapter on which my eyes should fall. For I had heard how one day Antony happened to go into a church while the gospel was being read and had taken it as a message for himself when he heard the words, 'Go and sell what you have, give it to the poor, and you will have a treasure in heaven; come, follow me.' And such an oracle had converted him to you.

Augustine, *Confessions* 8, 12

The Confessions

Opening prayer

Lord, you are great and infinitely worthy of praise. Great is your power and inscrutable your wisdom. Man is a puny part of your creation, and his desire is to praise you. He bears everywhere his mortality, the sign of his sin, to remind him that you resist the proud.

And yet this man desires to praise you, since he is a puny part of your creation.

It is you who bring him to seek joy in praising you, because you have made us for yourself and our heart is restless until it finds rest in you.

Grant me, Lord, to know and understand whether one should first call on you or praise you, and whether one must know you before calling on you. But who calls on you without knowing you? Someone who does not know you can always invoke another in your place. Rather, are you not called upon in order to be known? But 'how can they call on him in whom they do not believe?' And 'how will they believe unless they have a preacher?' 'Those who seek the Lord will praise him, and those who seek him shall find him', and 'those who find him will praise him . . .'

Who will grant me to rest in you? Who will grant me the sight of your entering my heart and filling it to the brim, so that I forget all the wrong I have done and embrace you alone, my one source of good?

What are you to me? Have pity on me, that I may speak. But what am I in your eyes, that you should command me to love you, and if I fail in this love you are angry with me and threaten me with great sorrow? Is it not already sorrow enough not to love you? Tell me in your mercy, O Lord my God, what you are for me. Say to my soul, 'I am your salvation.' Say that, in order that I may hear. The ears of my heart are before you, O Lord. Open them and say to my soul, 'I am your salvation.' I shall run after this voice and finally grasp you. Do not hide your face from me. Let me die – so as not to die – but let me see your face.

The abode of my soul is too small for you to enter; I pray you to enlarge it. It is in ruins; I pray you to repair it. It contains much that could shock your eyes: I know this and do not hide it. But who will purify it? There is no one but you to whom I can cry, 'Purge me, Lord, from my hidden sins; spare your saviour those offences which come from without.'

Augustine, *Confessions* 1, 1, 5

had joined the sect, thinking that he had found the solution there: an irreducible dichotomy. Ambrose and Neoplatonism detached him from it.

Donatism was the thorn in Augustine's episcopate. Since Cyprian, division had been rife, an endemic evil. After Diocletian's persecution, the election of Cecilian as primate of Carthage had been contested by the Numidian bishops. They had another candidate, Majorius. He was succeeded by Donatus. From then on the schism was complete, and was to spread from Carthage all over Africa.

Hippo was torn apart. There were two communities, two churches, two bishops. On Augustine's arrival the Donatists were in the majority and were giving the Catholics a hard time: the bakers even refused to bake bread for the orthodox. There was violence as well as tension and Augustine was ambushed. In addition to the conflict of authority there were also social and political consequences.

For twenty years Augustine made effort after effort, in debates and writings, returning constantly to unity in his preaching. In the end the Roman authorities intervened, and in 411 they called a conference, presided over by an imperial legate. Here 286 Catholic bishops and 279 Donatist bishops came together and put an end to the schism.

Pelagianism took up the last twenty years of Augustine's life. Pelagius was an ascetic monk who came from Ireland to Rome, where he reacted violently against the laxity of morals. He put the emphasis on human freedom, the resources of the will, so as to minimize the role of grace. The priest Celestius and Bishop Julian of Eclanum, 'great and subtle minds', backed up Pelagius and propagated, first in Africa and then in the East, a doctrine which was at the opposite extreme to Augustine's thought.

Augustine had been deeply affected by his spiritual experience, which had taught him that repentance was the victory of grace. For twenty years he heaped up work after work, filling two quarto volumes, to show the role of greed, the wretchedness of human beings when left to themselves, and then the doctrines of predestination and grace.

It is important not to reduce Augustine's work simply to controversy. He devoted his days to the community of Hippo and primarily to religious training. Teaching the word of God seemed to him to be the first and most important of his duties. He had incomparable gifts as an orator: warmth, sympathy, a lively manner, good imagery, the capacity to draw cameo sketches, skill at alliteration, proverbs, word-plays, and above all a knowledge of the human heart.

Augustine preferred to preach on scripture, mainly the Psalms and the Gospel of John; we have his commentaries on the Gospel. Some five hundred sermons survive; scholars estimate them to be a tenth of those he wrote. Augustine preached through the liturgical year and at festivals, developing the truths of the faith in a way which was understandable without being reductionist, and which never descended to facile moralism.

A born teacher, he laid the foundations for catechetical teaching in his *Catechesis for Beginners*, which has trained generations of teachers. In his *Christian Doctrine* he laid down the principles of what is now called homiletic.

Of all Augustine's work, his preaching is beyond question the part which has dated least. Through collections of homilies it has nourished the prayer, faith and Christian life of generations of monks and clergy down the centuries. Nowhere does the pastor express himself better, in solidarity with his people, 'a bishop for them, a Christian with them'.

3. The major works

Augustine's literary works comprise around one hundred titles, compositions of unequal length. Three which were constantly recopied and then published stand out: the *Confessions*, the *Treatise on the Trinity*, and *The City of God*. The three works are clearly very different, and they show the foundations of his genius.

The *Confessions* (397–401) are the most personal, the most novel, the most moving autobiographical work in antiquity. They show neither complacency nor self-justification. Rather, as is shown by the title, borrowed from the psalms, they are a confession of God and a confession of sin. 'To confess means to praise God and to accuse oneself.'

They are less a story than prayer and praise. Here we look in vain for personal confidences about a stormy youth. This is the most ardent hymn to the God who overturned his life, and we are deeply moved when reading it:

Late have I loved you,
beauty so old and so new,
late have I loved you.
You were within me
and I was outside.
There I sought you.
You touched me,
and your peace has burned me (10.38).

The *Treatise on the Trinity* is a work of his maturity; long meditated on (from 388–419), it was interrupted and then resumed. These reflections are an extension of the *Confessions* and keep within the confines of theology and mysticism. As the author acknowledges, they were begun in the prime of life, and completed in old age.

Augustine, like Hilary, was unconcerned about the Arian controversy, which hardly touched Africa. His approach is constructive. The first seven books expound trinitarian dogma in a somewhat arid way. After Book 8 the tone changes, and the text is transformed into a quest for traces of God in creation and in the tripartite structure of human beings (body, mind and spirit). Human beings bear within themselves a movement which is their principle and their end. Embryonic at creation, the image of God in us can be deformed, but cannot be lost. Renewed by grace, it is fulfilled in heavenly bliss, where 'God will open the last door, still held shut, on which I knock' (*On the Trinity* XV, 51).

To judge from the number of manuscripts of *The City of God* – more than four hundred – it has never ceased to provoke reflection down the centuries, at all the turning points of history. This is a meditation for apocalyptic times: the fall of Rome, which is its starting point, gradually takes on the dimensions of a theology of universal history.

Augustine worked on this book for fourteen years. The structure of the composition, which is often loose, indicates this. There are numerous digressions. Once more, the title is taken from the Psalms (86.3).

The theme, once begun, is later summed up in the succinct formula:

Two cities were created by two kinds of love:
the earthly city by self-love reaching the point of
*   contempt for God,*
the heavenly city by the love of God carried as far as
*   contempt of self (14.28).*

Though the themes are entangled and alternate, it is easy to distinguish in them the city of the earth and the city of heaven, and then the concrete realities of the church and the state, the people of God and the host of the impious. This basic theme is orchestrated and enriched with new harmonies, and extends to the dimensions of the world and history. 'Thus two cities, that of the impious and that of the saints, pursue their way from the beginning of the human race to the end of the world.'

The earthly city is only a figure, the shadow of the other city, which takes shape through time for pilgrims and which is to be found at the end of the way. 'Sing songs of love for your country,' says Augustine, 'a new way, a new traveller, a new song.'

In the *Soliloquies*, Augustine writes: 'I desire to know God and the soul. Nothing else? Truly, nothing.' These two questions, which are inextricably linked, remain basic for him. He does not cease to interrogate scripture and the church. Scripture is an instrument all of whose resources he knows, and it produces unexpected harmonies which he imitates, even to the point of rhythm and breathing.

The creative power of Augustine, his dialectical mind, served by the magic of the word, were not limited to rejuvenating a declining culture. His clearly new approach opened the way to a new civilization, mediaeval culture.

For the Rule of St Augustine, see p. 119.

Augustine's *City of God*,
incunabulum, Basel 1490

City of God: Preamble

The object of this work, my dear son Marcellinus, is the glorious city of God considered on the one hand as existing in this world of time, making its pilgrimage among the ungodly, living by faith, and on the other as it stands in its eternal dwelling place, waiting with patience for the day when justice is turned into judgment and, thanks to its holiness, it gains a supreme victory in perfect peace. I have undertaken it at your request, to fulfil the promise that I made to you to defend this city against those who prefer their own gods to its founder. It is a great and arduous task. But God is our helper.

I know what strength I need in order to demonstrate to the proud how powerful is the virtue of humility, a virtue which makes it soar above all the pinnacles of this world, which sway in their temporal instability, surpassing them all with an eminence which is not usurped by human pride but granted by divine grace. The king and founder of this city of which I have resolved to speak has revealed the decree of the divine law in the scriptures of his people: God resists the proud and gives his grace to the humble. But man's spirit, inflated with pride, seeks to appropriate this personal prerogative of God for itself, and delights to hear it said in its own praise that 'it spares the conquered and beats down the proud'.

It is, then, of the city of this world that I must speak, a city which seeks to dominate all, which holds nations in captivity but is dominated by a lust for rule. I must speak of this city, omitting nothing that the plan of this work demands and that my capacities allow.

Augustine, *City of God*, I, Preface

The Price of Love

Examine yourselves thoroughly, my brethren; destroy your inner granaries. Open your eyes, consider your capital of love, and increase what you have discovered in yourselves. Watch over this treasure so that you become rich in yourselves.

Those things are called dear which have a high price; this is no matter of chance. Note the expression 'this is dearer than that'. What does 'is dearer' mean? Does it not mean that it costs more? If one calls dearer all that costs more, what is dearer than love itself, my brethren? What do you think is its price? And how can that price be paid? The price of wheat is your copper; the price of a piece of land is your silver; the price of a stone, your gold; the price of your love, you. You want to buy a field, a stone, a beast of burden, and to pay for it you look for a piece of land, you look around you. But if you want to possess love, seek only yourself; find only yourself. What are you afraid of in giving yourself? Of losing yourself? But on the contrary, it is only in giving yourself that you will not lose yourself. Love itself is expressed in Wisdom and with a word calms the disarray into which the words 'Give yourself' cast you. For if a man wanted to sell you a field, he would say to you, 'Give me your gold', or if he were selling something else, 'Give me your copper, give me your silver.' Listen to what the mouth of Wisdom, love, tells you: 'My child, give me your heart. It was bad when it was in you, it was yours; you were prey to futility, to impure and baneful passions. Take it away from there. Where to? Where do you offer it? Give me your heart! Let it be mine, and you will not lose it. Look, has he wanted to leave anything in you which could make you still dear to yourself? 'You shall love the Lord your God,' he says, 'with all your heart and all your soul and all your thought.' What is left of your heart by which you could love yourself? What is left of your soul? And your thought? Everything, he says. He who made you asks you for everything. But do not be sorrowful, as if all joy were dead in you. Let Israel rejoice, not in itself but in him who made it.

Augustine, *Sermon* 34

Writers and Heresies of the Fourth and Fifth Centuries

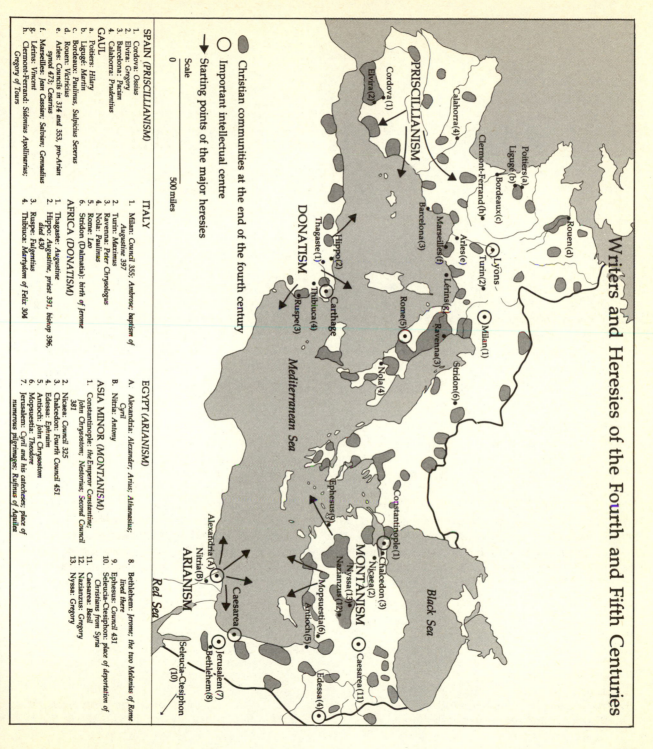

Legend:

- Christian communities at the end of the fourth century
- ◯ Important intellectual centre
- → Starting points of the major heresies

Scale
0 — 500 miles

SPAIN (PRISCILLIANISM)
1. Cordova: Ossius
2. Elvira: Gregory
3. Barcelona: Pacian
4. Calahorra: Prudentius

GAUL
a. Poitiers: Hilary
b. Ligugé: Martin
c. Bordeaux: Paulinus, Sulpicius Severus
d. Rouen: Victricius
e. Arles: Councils in 314 and 353, pro-Arian synod 473; Caesarius
f. Marseilles: Jean Cassian; Salvian; Gennadius
g. Lérins: Vincent
h. Clermont-Ferrand: Sidonius Apollinarius; Gregory of Tours

ITALY
1. Milan: Council 355; Ambrose; baptism of Augustine 397
2. Turin: Maximus
3. Ravenna: Peter Chrysologus
4. Nola: Paulinus
5. Rome: Leo
6. Stridon (Dalmatia): birth of Jerome

AFRICA (DONATISM)
1. Thagaste: Augustine
2. Nicaea: Council 325
3. Hippo: Augustine, priest 391, bishop 396, died 430
4. Chalcedon: Fourth Council 451
5. Edessa: Ephraim
6. Antioch: John Chrysostom
7. Ruspe: Fulgentius
8. Thibiuca: Martyrdom of Felix 304

EGYPT (ARIANISM)
A. Alexandria: Alexander; Arius; Athanasius;
B. Nitria: Antony

ASIA MINOR (MONTANISM)
1. Constantinople: the Emperor Constantine; John Chrysostom; Nestorius; Second Council 381
2. Nicaea: Council 325
3. Chalcedon: Fourth Council 451
4. Edessa: Ephraim
5. Antioch: John Chrysostom
6. Mopsuestia: Theodore
7. Jerusalem: Cyril and his catechises; place of numerous pilgrimages; Rufinus of Aquilea
8. Bethlehem: Jerome; the two Melanias of Rome lived there
9. Ephesus: Council 431
10. Seleucia-Ctesiphon: place of deportation of Christians from Syria
11. Caesarea: Basil
12. Nazianzus: Gregory
13. Nyssa: Gregory

Map labels:

PRISCILLIANISM
- Cordova (1)
- Elvira (2)
- Calahorra (4)
- Clermont-Ferrand (h)
- Poitiers (a)
- Liguge (b)
- Bordeaux (c)
- Rouen (d)
- Barcelona (3)
- Marseilles (f)
- Arles (e)
- Lérins (g)
- Lyons
- Turin (2)

DONATISM
- Thagaste (1)
- Hippo (2)
- Thibiuca (4)
- Ruspe (3)
- Carthage
- Rome (5)
- Milan (1)
- Ravenna (3)
- Stridon (6)
- Nola (4)

Mediterranean Sea

Red Sea

Black Sea

ARIANISM
- Alexandria (A)
- Nitria (B)
- Caesarea
- Jerusalem (7)
- Bethlehem (8)
- Edessa (4)
- Seleucia-Ctesiphon (10)

MONTANISM
- Constantinople (1)
- Chalcedon (3)
- Nicaea (2)
- Nyssa (13)
- Nazianzus (12)
- Caesarea (11)
- Ephesus (9)
- Mopsuestia (6)
- Antioch (5)

4

Towards Byzantinism
and the Middle Ages

With the Barbarian invasions, the fall of Rome and the decline of the late empire, a world died. Changes were to modify the map of East and West, which now separated. In this general upheaval the church became aware of its autonomy and its evangelizing mission. We have only to compare Salvian of Marseilles with Ambrose and Jerome to see the change of attitude.

The gulf between East and West seemed permanent. The Western empire had collapsed under Barbarian pressure. By contrast, the Christian East was experiencing a golden age. It made conquests in Africa, established itself in Ravenna and everywhere posed as the protector of the religion of Christ. For the East, an age of splendour was opening which was to last until the fall of Constantinople, New Rome, in 1453.

The progressive antagonism of the two halves of the empire was a burden on the unity of Christians, who from then on developed in two different cultural and even religious spheres. Theological controversies already fired only the regions which provoked them. Arianism and Nestorianism never mobilized the West, and Pelagianism remained foreign to the East. The patristic age survived in the East down to Byzantinism; Augustine is the precursor of the Middle Ages.

We have only to analyse and compare the last Greek and Latin writers to see the degree to which each breathes a different cultural atmosphere.

In each sphere the end of the patristic period comes at different dates. For the Latins, either Gregory the Great (died 604) or Isidore of Seville (died 636) is regarded as the last church father, but both are already mediaeval. In the East the patristic age is conventionally said to end with Cyril of Alexandria (died 444), but more often it is extended to John of Damascus (around 749), while patristic inspiration was to last until the end of Byzantinism.

I · The Latin West

The Barbarian invasions disrupted the Western church politically and culturally by breaking up its identity, its cohesion and its unity. The most notable effect of the upheaval was to cut the West off from its Hellenic sources. The movement began with Augustine, who was ill at ease in the Greek language and Greek thought (to the point of confusing the two Gregories), and became more marked, forcing the West to live in cultural self-sufficiency.

This break away from Greek roots went along with a literary and theological regionalization which intensified until Charlemagne reconstituted a new Christian West. The influx of pagan populations and Arian Barbarians made the church aware of the need for mission (as is evidenced by figures like Salvian of Marseilles, Cesarius of Arles and Gregory the Great). The evangelization of the countryside and the organization of rural parishes are visible signs of this.

The destruction of the cultural heritage by invasions, the dispersion of a large part of the intellectual élite, and the decay in the structures of public schools forced the churches and monasteries to fill the cultural gaps. The Christianization of culture begun by Augustine tended to become the privilege and mission of the clergy.

1. The vitality of Christian Gaul

Gaul occupied a more than distinguished place in the cultural geography of the West during the fifth and sixth centuries. Though invasions ravaged the countryside, the Christian populations began to regroup. The number of dioceses increased, above all south of the Loire, and councils met. The Bishop of Arles assumed a primacy and governed seven provinces, almost putting Rome in the shade.

The monasteries of Ligugé, Marmoutier, Rouen and then Marseilles and Lérins exercised an influence all over Gaul. The island of Lérins became the breeding ground of some remarkable bishops, who set out to evangelize, first the countryside and then the Barbarians when they had settled. The baptism of Clovis (497/508) at Reims, a historic date, was hailed as the advent of a new Constantine. It also marked the end of Romanism. Sidonius Apollinarius, Bishop of Clermont-Ferrand, a survivor of the Roman epoch, seemed to be living a century too late.

The focal points of interest for writers of the fifth and sixth centuries could be reduced to two: the monastic life and church history.

North Africa had known the religious life since the fourth century, but in Europe monasticism, inaugurated by Martin of Tours (died 397), developed intensively from the fifth century on, principally at Marseilles and on Lérins. John Cassian (360–430/35), one of the most remarkable writers of fifth-century Gaul, was to play a role of prime importance in it.

A Scythian by origin, with a Latin cultural background but perfectly at ease in Greek, John first spent long periods in Palestine, where he initiated himself into cenobitic life, and then among the monks of Egypt, where he met Moses and Paphnutius. He ended by settling in Marseilles, and founded two monasteries there, one for men and one for women (415/416). He was preoccupied with organizing Western monasticism, combining Eastern fervour with Latin moderation. He sought to integrate the essentials of anchoritic life into cenobitism.

Two books by Cassian form the charter of monastic life, the *Cenobitic Institutions*, a kind of introduction to the inner life, and the twenty-four *Conferences*, which are a complete presentation of spiritual doctrine, from the first purifications to perfection. All the monastic rules in East and West were inspired by it. John Cassian exercised a decisive influence on St Benedict and Cassiodorus.

Around 400, Honoratus installed a community of monks on the island of Lérins, near Cannes. The island rapidly became a centre of theological reflection for fifth-century Gaul and produced bishops for all the Rhone valley.

Two names stand out: Vincent of Lérins and Salvian of Marseilles. One book, the *Commonitorium* or Memorandum, was enough to ensure the fame of the monk Vincent of Lérins (died before 450). It is a kind of 'discourse on theological method', to distinguish faith from heresies. Its axiom has become famous: 'It is necessary to hold carefully to what is the object of faith, everywhere, always and for all' (see p. 112).

Salvian of Marseilles came from an aristocratic family. He was probably born in Trier, settled with

'Ubique et Semper': Everywhere and Always

But perhaps someone will say: 'So Christian doctrine is not capable of any progress in the church of Christ?' Certainly there has to be progress, indeed considerable progress. For who would be such an enemy of humanity, so hostile to God as to try to oppose it? But this progress must be true progress in the faith and not a change in it: progress means that each thing should grow while remaining itself, whereas change implies that one thing is turned into another.

Hence understanding, knowledge and wisdom must grow and advance widely, both in individuals and in the community, in a single person and in the church as a whole, according to ages and centuries. But they must progress precisely in accordance with their particular nature, that is, in accordance with the same kind of dogma, frame of mind and intellectual approach.

The development of religion in the soul should be like the development of the body. The body develops and extends its proportions over the years, yet constantly remains the same. Think of the difference between the prime of childhood and the maturity of old age. It is the same man who was once a youth and now is old; he is one and the same, though his figure and appearance have changed, and there remains within him one and the same nature, one and the same person. The limbs of infants at the breast are small, and those of young men are large, but they are the same. The very smallest have the same number of limbs as grown men, and though there are some which develop only in maturity, they already existed virtually in the embryo. Thus nothing new appears in old men which has not previously been latent in children.

So without any doubt the legitimate and correct rule of progress and the precise and impressive order of growth are observed when the course of years displays in human beings as they grow those parts and forms with which the wisdom of the Creator had previously endowed infants. If, however, the human form were later to take a form quite alien to its species, and if such a member were either removed or added, then the whole body would necessarily perish or become a monstrosity, or in any case would be seriously weakened.

These laws of progress must apply equally to Christian dogma: the years must consolidate it, time develop it and age make it more venerable; however, it should remain incorrupt and unimpaired, it should be complete and perfect in all the proportions of its parts and, shall we say, members, and in every sense that is proper to it. It does not allow any alteration, any loss of its specific character, or any variation of its defined form.

Vincent of Lérins, *Commonitorium*, 23

112

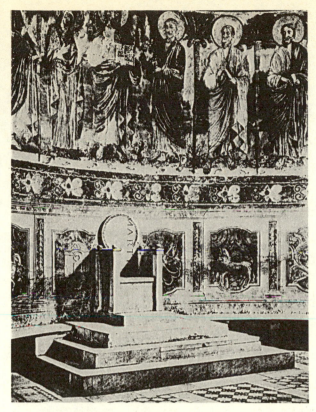

Cathedra of St Clement, Rome

his wife in the south of Gaul, and finally left his family to live on Lérins, near St Victor of Marseilles. According to the historian Gennadius, Salvian was a prolific author. In addition to letters, two works have come down to us: *To the Church*, a pamphlet against greed among Christians, including priests and bishops, and *The Divine Government*, a famous but controversial work.

Like Augustine in *The City of God*, Salvian witnessed the Barbarian wave breaking over Europe and contemplated the end of the Roman empire. The Jeremiah of the fifth century, he had a premonition of new times and attacked the Romans and the Gauls who were lamenting because they thought that God had abandoned the empire since it had become Christian.

Lérins also became established as a centre of education and evangelization. Eucherius, con-verted along with his wife to the religious life, entrusted the training of his two sons Salonius and Veranus to the monastery: the former became Bishop of Geneva, the latter Bishop of Vence. The island also provided a series of bishops for Arles (Honoratus, Hilary, Cesarius and Virgilius), for Riez (Maximus and Faustus), Lyons (Eucherius) and Troyes (Lupus). During the invasions these bishops defended their cities, sometimes at the cost of exile.

A generation later, Cesarius of Arles (470–543) was the most eminent bishop of that city, the 'Rome of Gaul', during the Barbarian invasions. He watched over church discipline and organized monastic life, writing two rules, one for men and one for women. He was beyond question the most popular preacher in Gaul. His 238 sermons, which often found a place alongside those of Augustine and circulated in numerous collections, were to nourish Christian generations from the Middle Ages to modern times (see p. 115).

History and hagiography are the second aspect of literature in Gaul. The *Life of Martin*, by Sulpicius Severus (360–420/25), was as popular as that of Antony. It became the model for hagiographies and the Golden Legend. Sulpicius also composed a *Universal Chronicle*, from the creation of the world to the year AD 400.

Gennadius of Marseilles (died 495/505) continued Jerome's *History of Famous Men*, providing a mine of information on the literary history of the fifth century. We have the end of his work *On the Heresies, The Book of Ecclesiastical Dogmas*.

Gregory of Tours (538–594) left a vast amount of hagiography more concerned with edification than historical exactitude. His vividly coloured *History of the Franks* shows his talent as a narrator. It is particularly valuable for the events to which Gregory was witness.

2. Papal action and the defence of culture in Italy

The majority of the bishops of Rome have left us letters, for the most part drafted by the pontifical chancellery. Leo the Great, who was pope from 440

113

to 461, has bequeathed us a considerable correspondence (123 letters) which bears the stamp of his style and his culture. He is one of the first popes to provide us with a set of sermons, ninety-six in all, mainly for liturgical festivals.

His phraseology is broad and majestic, moving on like a procession. The quality of his preaching lies less in the originality of his thought than in the elegance of his style, the sonority of his language and the liturgical beauty of its rhythm. He wanted to teach the truths of faith to his faithful.

A man used to government, Leo behaved like a king in Rome; he faced up to the invaders, like Attila, who retreated (452), and Genseric, king of the Vandals, who preserved the Eternal City in 455. Leo's *Letter to Flavian* laid the foundations for the Council of Chalcedon in 451. Leo was too Roman, too Western to be able to understand the complexity of the Christian East and prevent the development towards schism (see the text on p. 116).

A century later, two men in Italy were to struggle to maintain contact with the East and to preserve the cultural heritage, Boethius and Cassiodorus. Boethius (480–524), a Roman initiated into philosophy and Greek literature in Alexandria, was tragically halted in his project of translating Plato and Aristotle and executed on the orders of King Theodoric. He has bequeathed us his famous *Consolation of Philosophy*, written while he was in prison (text, p. 118).

The senator Cassiodorus, who at one time was head of the civil service, wrote two historical works (*Universal Chronicle, History of the Goths*). He finally retired to a private monastery at Vivarium, in

Conferences

The Christian is the branch which was cut from the root of Jesse and which after death comes more truly alive. All these things are covered by two cherubim, that is, by the plenitude of historical and spiritual knowledge. For cherubim denote abundance of knowledge. They ceaselessly cover the mercy-seat of God, namely the tranquillity of your heart, and protect it with their shadow against every attack of the evil spirits.

Thus your soul will be raised up to become not only the ark of the divine covenant but also a priestly realm, absorbed in some way with spiritual knowledge, and by its unfailing love of purity will fulfil the command given to the pontiff by the Lawgiver: 'He will not go forth from the sanctuary, lest he profane the sanctuary of God', that is to say his heart, where the Saviour promises that he will make his constant dwelling-place: 'I will live and walk among them.'

That is why we must be zealous to learn by heart the sequence of the Holy Scriptures and to commit them to memory constantly. This continual meditation will profit us in two ways. First, when the mind is occupied with reading and studying, evil thoughts have no way of taking the spirit captive in their toils. Then, it happens that when we have gone through certain passages a number of times in our efforts to commit them to memory, we have not had the time to understand them because our spirit did not have the necessary freedom. But once at a later stage we are free from the attraction of various occupations and the objects which fill our eyes, we can think them over in silence, above all during the night, and they will appear to us in a greater light. So it is with hidden meanings of which we did not have the slightest suspicion during our waking hours; it is when we are at rest, plunged so to speak into the lethargy of a heavy sleep, that understanding of them is revealed to us.

As our mind is renewed by this study, scripture too begins to take on a new face. A more mysterious understanding of them is given to us, and its beauty grows as we progress. For scripture adapts itself to the capacity of the human intelligence, being earthly to the carnal man and divine to the spiritual man. Thus those who once saw it as wrapped up in thick cloud find themselves unable either to grasp its depth or to endure its brilliance.

John Cassian, *Conferences* 14.10

How to Talk to the People

Bishops are said to be watchmen because they have been placed in a high position, as though on the top of the citadel of the church. Established before the altar, they should be solicitous for the city and the field of God, that is, the church. They must not only guard the great gates, that is, prohibiting mortal sin by salutary preaching, but also the little back doors and narrow entrances, that is, those venal errors which are committed every day. They must call for them to be wiped out by fasting, almsgiving and prayer . . .

The bishop may say, 'I am not eloquent and cannot explain Holy Scripture in this way.' But even if this is true, God does not require of us what we are unable to do. Bishops like this will not be esteemed the less, for even if a bishop possesses worldly eloquence, he must not preach with such language that he makes himself understood to only a minority of the faithful.

Can he not with his own eloquence make accessible and explain the obscurities of the Old and New Testaments, and indicate the depths of Holy Scripture? Certainly, if he so wills, he can censure adulterers and admonish the proud. What presbyter is there – I will not say bishop – who cannot say to his flock, 'Do not bear false witness, since scripture says, "The false witness shall not go unpunished." Do not lie, for it is written, "The mouth which lies kills the soul."'

Thus not only bishops in the cities but also priests and deacons in country parishes can and should preach often. Who is unable to say that no one should offer worship to trees, no one should observe omens, no one should resort to enchanters, no one should consider on what day he should leave his house and on what day return after the sacrilegious custom of the pagans. I fear that lay people and, what is worse, clergy succumb to this sacrilegious custom. Who cannot say, 'Let no one slander his neighbour if he does not want to be slandered, for "whoever speaks evil of his brother shall be destroyed"'? No one should hang phylacteries, diabolical magic signs or any kind of amulet on his clothing or that of his family, and no one should try to corrupt justice by seeking a bribe.

I do not know of any bishop, presbyter or even deacon who cannot preach in church and give all these and many other similar recommendations. Where an admonition in simple and popular language seems indispensable, neither eloquence nor great powers of memory are needed.

Does one have to be a scholar to say, 'Come to church in the morning, bring offerings to be dedicated on the altar, succour the sick, welcome the traveller, wash the feet of your guests, visit prisoners . . .'?

Cesarius of Arles, *Sermon* 1, 4, 12, 13

Calabria. There he collected a considerable library of Christian and secular authors and appointed religious to transcribe the texts. His *Institutions* gives directives for copying the manuscripts and contains a precise catalogue of the library.

By his dates the last of the Latin fathers, Pope Gregory the Great (540–604) came from a senatorial family. He was first of all prefect of Rome and then renounced the world to dedicate himself to the contemplative life. He was ordained deacon and then sent as a nuncio to Constantinople. He did not even learn Greek there. He was elected pope in 590 and gave to the world a perfect model of church government, as Bossuet remarked, administering

Jesus Christ: Two Natures, One Person

The whole body of the faithful profess that they believe in God the Father Almighty, and in Jesus Christ his only Son our Lord, who was born of the Holy Spirit and the Virgin Mary. These three statements are enough to conquer almost all heresies. For whoever believes God to be both Almighty and Father, also recognizes that the Son is everlasting together with him, differing in no way from him, because he is God from God, almighty from almighty, coeternal from eternal; not later in time nor inferior in power, not unlike him in glory nor divided from him in substance. But the same only-begotten, eternal Son of an eternal Father was born of the Holy Spirit and the Virgin Mary. This temporal birth in no way detracted from and in no way added to that divine and everlasting birth; it served solely to restore man who had been deceived by the devil, since the Son of God by his power was to conquer death and destroy the devil, who had the power of death. For we could not have overcome sin or the author of death had not he who could neither be contaminated by sin nor destroyed by death taken our nature upon himself and made it his own. So he was conceived of the Holy Spirit within the womb of a virgin mother who bore him, as she had conceived him, without loss of virginity.

Accordingly, the Son of God, descending from his throne in heaven and not departing from the glory of the Father, entered our poor world. He was born by a new order, a new mode of birth. It was a new order because the one who by nature is invisible became visible in ours; the one who could not be enclosed in space willed to be enclosed; the one who existed before time began to exist in time; the Lord of the universe allowed his infinite majesty to be overshadowed, and took upon himself the form of a slave; the impassible God did not disdain to be passible man, nor the immortal one to be subjected to the laws of death. And he was born by a new mode of birth, because inviolate virginity, knowing nothing of lust, supplied the flesh of the Son of God. The Lord took his nature from his mother; but for all that he assumed no fault, nor does the wondrousness of the nativity of our Lord Jesus Christ, born of a Virgin's womb, mean that his nature is unlike ours. For he who is very God is also very man, and there is no lie in this union, for it is formed of the lowliness of man and the loftiness of God. Just as God is not changed by the compassion which is shown, so man is not consumed by the divine dignity. Each of the two natures works in union with the other that which is proper to it; thus the Word performs that which pertains to the Word, and the flesh carries out that which pertains to the flesh. The one of these shines out in miracles and the other succumbs to injuries. And as the Word does not withdraw from equality with the Father in glory, so, too, the flesh does not abandon the nature of our kind. For as we must keep saying, he is one and the same, truly Son of God, and truly Son of Man.

Leo, *Letter to Flavian* 2, 4

the rich heritage of the Roman church which was to become the 'papal states'. He tried to impose his authority all over the Christian world and was also concerned enough to send a missionary monk, Augustine, to England. His correspondence is considerable (850 letters).

Despite precarious health to which he refers in his preaching, Gregory devoted himself to his apostolic task with fervour, learning from Cyprian and above all from Augustine. His *Homilies on the Gospels* indicate the quality of his inner life and the concern of his pastoral action in simple and popular language.

His moral commentaries on the book of Job and his homilies on Ezekiel, addressed to monks, along with his *Pastoral Rule*, the priest's bedside book, are classics. They were the most copied books in the Middle Ages, and could be found in all respectable mediaeval libraries. Gregory restricted his exegesis to allegory and spiritual considerations. With him the Middle Ages were born.

3. The Iberians and the Visigoths

Roman Spain produced several distinguished writers, like Bishop Pacian of Barcelona (died before 392); Gregory of Elvira, his contemporary, an admirable theologian and exegete; Orosius (who died after 418), whose *History against the Pagans* is rather limited; Apringius (died 551), who composed a *Commentary on the Apocalypse*; and Martin of Braga (515–89), a monk become bishop who knew Greek and was one of the most cultivated figures of his time.

Isidore (560–636), Bishop of Seville in the Visigothic period, is often considered the last of the church fathers. He is one of the principal architects of a cultural renewal. He had an encyclopaedic mind and edited the *Etymologies*, a compilation of all the secular and religious knowledge of his time. It was one of the most read and also the most copied books in the Middle Ages, of which it was the precursor in its approach.

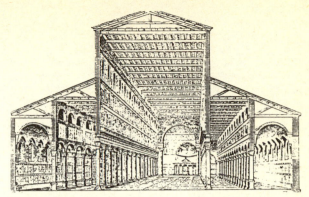

Constantinian basilica of St Peter of the Vatican

Advice from Pope Gregory the Great to Augustine, Missionary Monk in England (601)

The least possible number of pagan temples are to be destroyed; let only the idols which are in them be destroyed; let them be sprinkled with blessed water; let altars be built and relics placed there. Thus, if the temples are well built, the change will be only to their use: whereas formerly this was the cult of demons, now it is the worship of the true God. And in this way the people, seeing that its places of worship have not been destroyed, will forget its errors and, having come to the knowledge of the true God, will come to worship him in the very places where their ancestors gathered. And as they are accustomed to sacrifice many oxen in honour of devils, no changes should be made to their customs on feast days: for example, on the anniversary of the dedication or on the festivals of the holy martyrs whose relics lie in the church, let them make booths of boughs around the churches as they used to do round pagan temples, and let them celebrate the festival by religious banquets . . . In thus allowing them to express their joy outwardly, you will lead them more easily to know an inner joy, since it is impossible to cut off everything at once from hearts which are so obdurate. One does not climb a mountain by leaps and bounds, but with slow steps.

Letters XI, 56, quoted in Bede,
Ecclesiastical History, Chapter XXX

The Consolation of Philosophy

In the same way, the mists of sadness dissolved, I returned to the daylight and recovered my senses, so that I could recognize the one who was looking after me. So turning my eyes towards her and fixing my gaze on her, I saw once again my nurse Philosophy, in whose house I had dwelt since my youth. 'Why,' I cried, 'O mistress of all the virtues, have you left the heights of heaven to come into this wilderness of my exile? Have you come to keep me company in being falsely accused?'

'Would I forsake you,' she replied, 'and not share in the burden that you bear because of the hatred of my name, dividing the labour with you? It was never right for Philosophy to forsake the innocent in his trouble and leave him without a companion. Should I fear any accusations, as though this were something new? Do you think that this is the first time that wisdom has been exposed to danger by wicked men? Did I not in ancient times, before the age of my disciple Plato, wage a great combat with the rashness of folly? And while Plato was alive, did not his master Socrates win the victory of an unjust death in my presence? Then, one after the other, the mob of Epicureans, Stoics and all the rest launched an attack on my heritage, each in their own way, dragging me towards them in spite of my cries and my efforts, in order to have me as part of their plunder. They tore the garment which I had woven with my own hands, and having seized some small pieces of it, thinking that I was wholly in their grasp, they departed. Because certain signs of my clothing appeared on some of them, they were rashly thought to be my familiar friends, and condemned through the error of the profane multitude. And if you have not heard of the exile of Anaxagoras, the poison of Socrates or the torture of Zeno, because all that happened in foreign lands, at least you may know of Canius, Seneca and Soranus, whose memory is neither ancient nor obscure. What led them to ruin if not that they had been trained in my discipline and were not to the liking of the taste of wicked men? So you have no cause to marvel if in the sea of this life we are tossed with boisterous storms, the main purpose of which is to displease the wicked. Certainly there is a great host of them, but it is to be despised, because it is not governed by any leader, but is carried up and down by rash error which lacks any order. And if at any time they attack us with great strength, then reason our master withdraws her troops into the citadel, and the enemy has nothing to do but plunder unimportant baggage.'

Boethius, *Consolation of Philosophy*, Book I, 3

Like St Basil, St Augustine was a bishop: when he addresses the religious, he first of all maintains his pastoral concern.

The Rule of St Augustine is also the one with the most communal character; it stresses sharing more than detachment, brotherly communion and harmony more than chastity and obedience. The presence of scripture is constant here, even if it is not very explicit; critical editions have counted more than two hundred evocations of or allusions to the Bible, quite apart from explicit references.

Since the edition of the works of St Augustine made by the Maurists, the Rule has been included in his correspondence: it comprises letter CCXI, thought to have been written in 423 to women religious who wanted to change their superior; St Augustine calls them to concord.

Paragraphs 1–4 of this letter seem to have been a rebuke, while paragraphs 5–10 (given below) may be the feminine version of what could have been originally a masculine rule, the Praeceptum, *which Augustine produced around 397 for the lay monastery of Hippo. Modern scholars are undecided as to whether the rule was first drawn up for men or women.*

Rule of St Augustine

The rules which we lay down to be observed in the monastery are these:

First of all, since you are gathered under the same roof, dwell there in a perfect union. Let your hearts and minds be one in God. Have nothing of your own, but let all things be common property among you. Your superior must distribute food and clothing to each of you – not equally to all, because you are not equally strong, but to each one according to her need. For we read in the Acts of the Apostles: 'They had all things in common and distribution was made to each according to their need.' Let those of you who had any worldly goods when they entered the monastery allow them to become common property. And let those who had no worldly goods not seek to have in the community what they could not have had while they were outside its walls, but let them be given what they need in accordance with their infirmity, though they may have been so poor in the world that they could not have found the bare essentials of life. However, they should not reckon as the main blessing of their present lot that they have found in the community food and clothing which they lacked before they were received into it.

Let them not hold their heads high in pride because they are associated with others whom they would not have dared to approach in the outside world; rather let them lift their hearts on high. Let them not seek after earthly goods, for fear that the monasteries may become useful only to the rich and not to the poor, which would happen if they were a place of humbling for the rich and pride for the poor. On the other hand, let not those who have some status in the world scorn those who, poor though they were, have become their sisters in a holy union. Let them not glory in the dignity and wealth of their parents, but in the society of their poor companions. And let them not give themselves airs because they have contributed to the wellbeing of the community, and let them not become more proud of the riches that they have given to the monastery than if they were enjoying them in the world. The other vices find scope in evil works, but pride lurks even in good works and makes them of no avail. What is the use of distributing one's goods among the poor and becoming poor oneself if the soul takes more pride in scorning riches than in possessing them? Live then, all of you, in unanimity and concord, and in each other give honour to the God whose temple you have been made.

Pray at the appointed hours and times. Let no one for whatever reason change the use of the oratory, the name of which alone shows that it is a place of prayer, so that if some sisters want to go there to pray between the appointed hours they may not be hindered by others using the place for some other purpose. When you use psalms and hymns in your prayers, let your heart feel what your lips are saying; sing only that which ought to be sung, and content yourselves with saying the rest in a low voice.

Keep your flesh subdued by fasting and abstinence from food and drink, always so far as your health allows. When one among you is not able to fast, unless she be sick, let her not take any nourishment outside the ordinary mealtimes. When you are at table, until you rise from it, listen without noise and disputation to whatever may be being read to you, so that not only does your mouth receive food but your ears also receive the word of God.

Augustine, *Letter* 211, 5–8

II · The Christian East

The first striking thing in the East is the continuity between the fifth and sixth centuries and the age which preceded them. The periods follow on harmoniously, with no break between antiquity and the Middle Ages. Over against the scattered West stood the monolithic power of the emperor, the *basileus*. Justinian, heir to Constantine and Theodosius, was concerned to reconquer the empire for Christ.

The emperor felt responsible before God for both the spiritual and the temporal well-being of the Christian people. Hence the interpenetration of the two powers to the point that the emperor nominated and deposed bishops and patriarchs at will. The authority of the prince weighed heavily on the decisions of the Second Council of Constantinople in 553. Justin had the formidable advantage of being a competent theologian.

The Byzantine theologians were aware of being an extension of the theological and cultural tradition of former centuries, and drawing on the same scriptural and patristic sources.

The *Catenae* (chains), commentaries on scripture with the aid of patristic quotations, exploited the same heritage. So in the East the situation was more one of maturity than of decadence. The two councils of Ephesus and Chalcedon gave a clear response, the former to Nestorianism by affirming the unity of Christ, and the latter to Monophysitism, attesting the two distinct natures in Jesus. However, these councils did not put an end to the controversies, which reappeared in new forms, like Monotheletism, perpetuating themselves and becoming crystallized. From now on the Eastern churches were divided between Monophysites and Nestorians.

In the East, monasticism continued to serve as a catalyst, so as to maintain the purity and rigour of the gospel in a lukewarm society, to support the economy of rural populations, and to give them social assistance in the form of diaconia. Monasticism developed a spiritual theology deriving from

Origen, though the theologian himself remained a source of discord. There was a dispute which ended by condemning Origenist theses at the Council of Constantinople (553).

Four men deserve special mention: Pseudo-Dionysus, Romanus the Melodist, Maximus Confessor and John of Damascus.

1. Pseudo-Dionysus

An anonymous author of the end of the fifth and beginning of the sixth centuries hid himself so well behind the pseudonym of Dionysus the Areopagite that researches so far have failed to identify him. Syrian by origin, a disciple of Neo-Platonism and Proclus, and dependent on Gregory of Nyssa, Pseudo-Dionysus wrote works the chief of which form a group of four: the *Divine Names*, the *Mystical Theology*, the *Celestial Hierarchy*, and the *Ecclesiastical Hierarchy*.

These works analyse in turn the attributes of God, the first cause and the end of all things. God is surrounded by the hierarchy of heavenly spirits, grouped into triads and reproduced in the church by the three sacraments of initiation, the three degrees of ministries and the three states of life (monks, faithful, imperfect). The *Mystical Theology* describes the ascent to God, to the point of ecstatic contemplation.

This corpus of writing was translated into Latin fourteen times in the West, after Hilduin (833) and above all John Scotus Erigena (858) had made it known. It was a fertile source for all mediaeval theology, from the Victorines to St Thomas and St Bonaventure and up to the mystics of the Rhineland, and gave them access to the theological legacy of the East.

2. Romanus the Melodist (died 556)

The contribution of Romanus the Melodist, who was born at Emesa and died at Constantinople, is principally poetical and liturgical. He must have composed around a thousand hymns, some of which are used in the Byzantine liturgy. The most famous is certainly the *Akathistos* ('sung standing'), in honour of the Virgin. It is a classic of Christian poetry.

3. Maximus the Confessor (580–666)

Maximus is the most important Greek theologian of the seventh century, the last original and creative thinker of the Byzantine church.

After a public career he was converted to the monastic life and fought effectively against Monotheletism (which accepted only one will in Christ). However, he was condemned at the Lateran Council and died in exile.

A fertile author, eclectic in his Greek sources (Aristotle and Neoplatonism), he wrote eleven *Dogmatic Treatises and Letters* against Monotheletism. Of his ascetical works, mention should be made of the *Liber Asceticus*, *Four Centuries on Charity*, and the *Mystagogy*, which traces the way to perfection.

4. John of Damascus (640–753)

John came from Damascus and is deemed to bring the patristic era to an end. Originally a high-ranking imperial dignitary, he eventually retired to the monastery of St Sabas, near Jerusalem, which still exists today. There he is buried, after living for more than a century.

The *Source of Knowledge*, the best known of his writings, was often translated into Latin. In three parts, it provides an initiation into philosophy, a history of heresies and finally a synthetic account of Christian faith which quotes the Greek fathers abundantly.

Three Discourses on Images demonstrate that this cult is well founded. The *Sacred Parallels*, so called because in it vices and virtues are treated in pairs, may have been composed by him. They provide a vast anthology of more than five thousand texts, drawn from scripture and the fathers, paving the way for numerous Damascene anthologies which are derived from it.

Romanus the Melodist: Hymn on the Passion

The tyranny of hatred is broken, the tears of Eve are dried by your passion, friend of men, Christ God: in it, death is regenerated; through it, the robber finds a refuge. Adam alone exults.

1

Be struck dumb, heaven, today! Earth, plunge into chaos! Do not venture, sun, to look at your master on the cross where he hangs of his own free will! Let the rocks split asunder, for the rock of life is being murdered at this moment by the nails. Let the veil of the temple be rent asunder, since the body of the Lord has been pierced with a lance by criminals. At last all creation trembles, groans, before the passion of the creator: Adam alone exults.

2

Saviour, you have taken my condition that I may achieve yours. You have accepted the passion so that now I may scorn the passions; your death has restored me to life. You were put in the tomb, and through your sojourn you have made me the gift of paradise. By descending to the depths of the abyss you have exalted me; by beating on the gates of hell you have reopened to me the gates of heaven. Yes, you have suffered because of the fallen, you have endured all for the exultation of Adam.

The Second Century

1. The man who truly loves God also does not allow anything to distract him when he prays; and the man who does not allow anything to distract him when he prays also truly loves God. But the man who has his mind fixed on some earthly thing does not love God.

2. The mind which dwells on something of the senses certainly feels a passion for that thing, such as desire, or grief, or anger, or ill-will. And unless it scorns that thing, it cannot be freed from such a passion.

3. When the passions control a mind, they fix it on material things and, keeping it from God, lead it to occupy itself with these things. But if the love of God is stronger, it delivers the mind from such bonds and persuades it to scorn not only the things of the senses, but even this transitory life.

4. The work of the commandments is to make the thought of things simple. The work of reading and contemplation removes the mind from all matter and all form. Through it we can achieve undistracted prayer.

5. The active way is not sufficient to free the understanding completely from the passions so that it can pray undistracted, unless various spiritual contemplations follow it. The active way frees the mind only from intemperance and hate; the others take it away from forgetfulness and ignorance. And thus it will be able to pray as it ought.

6. There are two supreme states of pure prayer, one for those with an active life, the other for contemplatives. One is born of the fear of God and a good hope, the other from divine love and extreme purification. The signs of the first state are these: when the mind withdraws from all thoughts of the world, as though God himself were beside it – as indeed he is – it prays without allowing itself to be distracted or troubled. The sign of the second is that at the very beginning of prayer the mind is ravished by the infinite light of God; it loses all sense of itself and no longer feels any other being except the one who through love brings about such illumination in it. Then, being drawn towards the divine reason, it receives pure and clear images of God.

7. A man clings totally to what he loves and scorns all that is opposed to it, so as not to be deprived of it. The man who loves God applies himself to pure prayer and casts out of himself every passion that prevents him from praying.

8. The man who casts out egotism, self-love, the mother of the passions, will easily with God's help put away the others like anger, grief, resentment, and so on. But the one who is seized by the first passion is wounded, though against his will, by the second. Self-love is the passion that one has for the body.

9. There are five reasons why people love one another, whether to their praise or their blame: either for the love of God, as the virtuous man loves everybody and as the man who is not yet virtuous loves the virtuous man; or for natural reasons, as parents love their children and vice versa; or for vain glory, as the man who is extolled loves the one who extols him or for love of money, as one loves a wealthy man for benefits received; or for love of pleasure, as the man who cares only for his belly and for sex. The first reason is praiseworthy, the second is mediocre, the rest are marked by passion.

10. If you hate some people and neither love nor hate others, while others you love moderately, and yet others you greatly love, this inequality shows you that you are far from perfect love, which supposes that one should love each person equally.

11. 'Turn away from evil and do good.' That is to say, fight against your enemies to reduce the patterns; then, keep sober so that they do not increase. Fight to acquire virtues, and then be sober and vigilant in order to keep them.

12. Those whom God has allowed to tempt us, either arouse the desires of the soul or trouble its ardour; they darken our reason or fill the body with pain or take from that which it has.

13. The demons either tempt us by themselves or by arming those who have no fear of the Lord to be against us: by themselves, when we are alone apart from others, as they tempted the Lord in the wilderness; by men, when we associate with others as the Lord was tried by the Pharisees. But let us, looking towards our model, repel them no matter how they come.

Maximus the Confessor, *The Four Centuries on Charity*, II, 1–13

Conclusion

A look back at the patristic period shows clearly enough that here we have fully developed thought, implemented in action, by responsible pastors of churches. Hence the priority given to preaching and evangelization. This is obvious from the two most amazing geniuses, Origen and Augustine.

This primacy of pastoral action characterizes both East and West, but in different ways. If we analyse it schematically, the genius of Eastern writers is intuitive, speculative, lyrical and mystical; that of the West is legal, pragmatic, moral and compact. The Greek writers put the emphasis on the greatness of human beings; African and Iberian theologians put it on their failure (with the exception of Tertullian). The former develop the divinization of Christians, the latter their retribution. From there we would also have to go on to make further distinctions, between individuals and between geographical and cultural settings.

The movement of events, human shortsightedness and passion, and the course of politics gradually cracked the one holy church, and tore its seamless robe. The drama, for a while limited to Africa, spread throughout the church, cut off the East from the West, and finally impoverished all the disciples of Christ, who from then on have been in search of a lost unity.

As Fr de Lubac once remarked, there can be no renewal or depth in the church without a study of its sources, primarily the church fathers. If that is the case, we can say that today there is a renewal in the church to the degree that we can note a revival of patristic studies. This revival may be timid and localized, but it is real.

If we ask why there is this interest in the fathers, at a time when there is perhaps a decline in scholastic studies, I think that we can discover several reasons.

1. The fathers are close to the beginnings

This first point is very important. The fathers are closer to Christian origins than we are. This is not just a chronological proximity but also a psychological and cultural proximity. Many Greek fathers, above all, inhabit the cultural milieu of the Bible. They speak the Greek of the New Testament. One has only to read the Latin and Greek commentaries on the Lord's Prayer to see the finesse and the precision with which John Chrysostom or Theodore of Mopsuestia read the Greek text of the New Testament. Neither understands a clause of the Lord's Prayer as the Latins translate it, 'Forgive us our trespasses as we forgive', but in accordance with the Greek text, which has an aorist: 'Forgive us our trespasses as we have forgiven those who trespass against us.' A whole theology stems from this difference in translation.

What disconcerts us when we read the Bible and

the fathers is the cultural difference between our time and this past time. That problem did not arise for the fathers. For that reason, their commentaries on scripture continue to be of great interest to us. The Greek of the New Testament is the language that they speak and feel, and the cultural milieu of Paul is known to Basil of Caesarea and John Chrysostom.

2. The fathers are pastors

The fathers did not write to give us material for doctoral theses but to teach, guide and correct their flock. I think that by contrast the mediaeval masters induce a degree of lassitude because they developed their theology in university laboratories.

By contrast, almost all the fathers are bishops. If we ignore the polemic necessitated by controversy, their writings are sermons, exhortations, letters to guide and illuminate their faithful. Hence their direct tone, their existential doctrine, preoccupied not with constructing a good system but with helping souls to find the way of salvation.

Let us take St Augustine as an example. Here is a speculative thinker who, once converted, asked only for solitude in order to pray, reflect and write. God wanted otherwise. Against his will, Augustine became a priest and then Bishop of Hippo. The greater part of the life of this exceptional genius was devoted to his small flock in Hippo. His work as a bishop was overwhelming: preaching, catechesis, administration, the tribunal. That was his everyday work.

What was he to do? Was he on the one hand to write learned books and on the other to popularize them for lesser mortals, offering a little moralizing sermon? No, he tried to put all theology, including the mystery of the Trinity, within the reach of these ordinary people. For there are not two weights and two measures; there is not a theology for the scholars and a faith for simple people, but one revelation which is primarily addressed to the 'lowly and humble'.

This direct and concrete theology, open to everyone, which is the fruit of spiritual experience rather than speculation, is a wealth which makes patristics

worth its weight in gold. This wealth of life and spiritual experience that we find in Hilary and above all in Gregory of Nyssa marks out the way to all theological reflection and all sacramental life, guiding them towards spiritual and mystical experience.

3. The fathers belong to an ecumenical church

There is another element of which we are particularly aware today, now that we are again taking the ecumenical problem seriously. That is, that the fathers bear witness to a church which is still one. The church of Ambrose and Gregory of Nazianzus is neither Greek nor Latin; it is the church. We can see how from East to West all the Latin fathers up to Augustine, who marks the opening of another stage, read and use the rich Greek heritage. Look at the influence exercised by Origen on Ambrose, who often paraphrases the Greek thinker.

This permanent sharing relates not only to texts and books but also to events. There was no emergency, calamity in the East for which Rome did not offer aid. We still have the letter of congratulations from Basil when he learned that Ambrose had been nominated to the see of Milan. The same current, the same life, ran from Ravenna and Lyons to Alexandria and Antioch, passing through Carthage and Constantinople.

The East brought its own riches, its more philosophical vocabulary, its more ontological theological presentation, its more optimistic conception of the faith. The West is more legalistic, and draws on the language of law in forging its theological terminology. Latin thought is less speculative and more concrete, more moral and also more pessimistic, as is evident above all from the Pelagian crisis. Here we have different temperaments, and this variety, which gives patristic thought its richness, always respects the unity and integrity of one and the same faith.

All this teaches us 'the effort of bold creation', which is the condition for real spiritual fruitfulness.

It is clear that the Latin church impoverished itself terribly in every respect – theologically, spiritually and liturgically – by cutting itself off from the East. We only have to recall Vatican II and the disquiet of the Eastern Catholic bishops to see how the West ended up acting, reflecting and sometimes legislating in a local and regional rather than a universal and ecumenical way. There is no route to reunion with our Orthodox brothers which does not lead through a deepening of this common heritage, this expansion of our Western horizon eastwards.

Here is a simple example. Relatively recently, our missionaries have imposed on Africa a liturgy which is ill-suited to the sensitivity of these peoples and their modes of expression, when on the same continent of Africa since the second century there has been an 'African' liturgy, well suited and well tried, in Ethiopia. We need recall only this. It is often said that the English and French are bad at geography. But they are not the only ones.

Peacocks on a lead seal found in Tunisia

For Further Reading

This bibliography is meant to take the reader just one step further, and is limited to books which are easily accessible. Most of the titles listed here contain bibliographies themselves, some annotated.

Further introduction

Those wanting to know more about the church fathers will find the *Oxford Dictionary of the Christian Church*, second edition, Oxford University Press 1974, a veritable treasure trove (a third edition is in preparation for 1993 or 1994). Jean Comby, *How to Read Church History*, Volume 1, SCM Press and Crossroad Publishing Company 1985, makes an ideal companion volume to *How to Read the Church Fathers*. See also Boniface Ramsey, *Beginning to Read the Fathers*, Darton, Longman and Todd 1986; Maurice Wiles, *The Christian Fathers*, SCM Press 1977.

Reference

B. Altaner, *Patrology*, Nelson 1960
J. Quasten, *Patrology*, Christian Classics 1983 (three volumes)

A 'patrology' gives details of the fathers whom it covers, summarizing their life and work and giving detailed bibliographies.

Texts

(a) Selections

Henry Bettenson (ed.), *The Early Christian Fathers*, Oxford University Press 1956 (from Clement of Rome to Athanasius)
Henry Bettenson (ed.), *The Later Christian Fathers*, Oxford University Press 1970 (from Cyril of Jerusalem to Leo the Great)
J. Stevenson and W. H. C. Frend, *A New Eusebius*, SPCK ²1987 (documents relating to thought and history to AD 337)

J. Stevenson and W. H. C. Frend, *Creeds, Councils and Controversies*, SPCK ²1989 (documents relating to thought and history from 337–461)

Maurice Wiles and Mark Santer (eds.), *Documents in Early Christian Thought*, Cambridge University Press 1975

Fortress Press, Minneapolis publish a series 'Source of Early Christian Thought' which bring together material from the fathers on certain specific topics. See especially:
William Rusch (ed.), *The Trinitarian Controversy*, 1980
R. A. Norris, Jr, *The Christological Controversy*, 1980
J. Patout Burns, *Theological Anthropology*, 1981
E. Glenn Hinson, *Understandings of the Church*, 1986

(b) Collections

During the nineteenth century two major collections of patristic writings were published: the Ante-Nicene Christian Fathers and Nicene and Post-Nicene Christian Fathers. These have been reissued and are still available from Eerdmans, Grand Rapids, Michigan. All the major works of the relevant major fathers are represented, but readers should be warned that the nineteenth-century English is often difficult to follow. For that reason many people will prefer two more recent series: Ancient Christian Writers, Paulist Press; Fathers of the Church, Universities of America Press. Some works are also available in the Oxford University Press series Oxford Early Christian Texts. The Loeb Classical Library, Harvard University Press, publishes some patristic works: these volumes have the Greek or Latin text with translation on a facing page. Both Philo and Josephus are well represented here.

Those who can read French are infinitely better off. The magnificent series *Source chrétiennes*, published by Editions du Cerf, was begun in 1941 and now numbers more than 350 volumes, all with texts, translations and notes.

Histories and general accounts

A. Grillmeier, *Christ in Christian Tradition*, Mowbray 1975

S. G. Hall, *Doctrine and Practice in the Early Church*, SPCK 1991

J. N. D. Kelly, *Early Christian Creeds*, Longman ³1972

J. N. D. Kelly, *Early Christian Doctrines*, A. & C. Black ⁵1989

Frances Young, *From Nicaea to Chalcedon*, SCM Press and Fortress Press 1983 (contains an exhaustive bibliography of works in English)

Francis Young, *The Making of the Creeds*, SCM Press and Trinity Press International 1991 (the most approachable general account)

Works on and by individual writers
(in alphabetical order)

The Apologists

R. M. Grant, *Greek Apologists of the Second Century*, Westminster/John Knox Press and SCM Press 1988

The Apostolic Fathers (Barnabas, Clement, Didache, Ignatius, etc.)

Early Christian Writings, Penguin Books ²1987

Arius

Rowan Williams, *Arius: Heresy and Tradition*, Darton Longman and Todd 1987

Athanasius

On the Incarnation, Mowbray and St Vladimir's Seminary 1944 (with an introduction by C. S. Lewis)

Augustine

Peter Brown, *Augustine of Hippo*, Faber 1967 (a classic!)

Henry Chadwick, *Augustine*, Past Masters, Oxford University Press 1986

City of God, Penguin Books ²1983

Confessions, Penguin Books 1961
Oxford University Press 1992 (by Henry Chadwick)

Eusebius

History of the Church, Penguin Books 1965

Gnosticism

Bentley Layton (ed.), *The Gnostic Scriptures*, Doubleday and SCM Press 1988

James M. Robertson, *The Nag Hammadi Library in English*, E. J. Brill ³ 1988

Jerome

J. N. D. Kelly, *Jerome*, Duckworth 1975

Justin

L. W. Barnard, *Justin Martyr*, Cambridge University Press 1967

Origen

H. Crouzel, *Origen*, T. & T. Clark 1989

J. W. Trigg, *Origen*, John Knox Press and SCM Press 1987

Index of Extracts quoted in Boxes

Index of Names

(This index is limited to listing the main authors and anonymous documents mentioned in the book)